ADVANCE PRAISE
BEAUTY OF MOTHERHOOD

"You will not meet more tender guides for your mothering journey than Kim Knowle-Zeller and Erin Strybis. A beautiful blend of story, application, and prayer, *The Beauty of Motherhood* is a master class in experiencing God in the everyday moments of motherhood. These pages are soaked in love, glimmering with grace, and will surely be a gift to mothers everywhere."—**Ashlee Gadd, Founder of *Coffee + Crumbs* and author of *The Magic of Motherhood: The Good Stuff, the Hard Stuff, and Everything In Between* and *Create Anyway: The Joy of Pursuing Creativity in the Margins of Motherhood***

"These poignant and prayerful meditations will bring you back to yourself—and the love God has for you and your children. The spiritual reflections and soulful prayers in this book affirm what many of us know to be true: on our wonderful, messy mothering journeys, we experience God in new ways. I'm grateful for the depth Erin Strybis and Kim Knowle-Zeller bring to these chapters, which are short enough for us to receive even in our most depleted moments. May their words care for your soul as you care for your family." —**Kayla Craig, creator of Liturgies for Parents and author of *To Light Their Way: A Collection of Prayers & Liturgies for Parents***

"Erin Strybis and Kim Knowle-Zeller share their deep intimate reflections of motherhood with profound tenderness. While reading, I found myself thinking of my own children while also imagining my mother as a young woman, cradling me in her arms decades ago. Certainly, no single devotional can address every aspect of motherhood. Yet, Knowle-Zeller and Strybis provide a poignant, compassionate devotional for young moms that is inspirational and honest."—**The Rev. Angela T. !Khabeb, ELCA Pastor, *Living Lutheran* columnist, Public Theologian, and *Good Morning America* guest contributor**

"Where was this book when my children were young? In an easy-to-read, invitational style, the authors of *The Beauty of Motherhood* share a myriad of true-life stories that cover the messy, the mundane, and the marvelous moments of being a mom. Readable, relatable, and real, the stories are woven together with prayers, scripture, ponderings, and practices that combine to make this book an inspiring, perfect gift for any mom. Simply lovely."—**Glenys Nellist, author of *God Made Mommy Special* and *The Wonder That Is You***

"With honesty and wit, Kim Knowle-Zeller and Erin Strybis offer mothers stories that will encourage, restore, inspire, and convict. They turn doubt and worry into faith and hope, sadness and frustration into gratitude and joy. Knowle-Zeller and Strybis look to and write about parenting challenges with a faith and a love that will fill mothers' souls so that they in turn may attend to the souls of those they've been called to mother."—**Callie R. Feyen, author of *The Teacher Diaries: Romeo & Juliet* and *Twirl: My Life with Stories, Writings & Clothes***

"When a new baby is born, a new mother is also born, whether it is her first child or her seventh. With gentle yet incisive wisdom, Erin Strybis and Kim Knowle-Zeller invite mothers into the beautiful, personal story that God is writing through their parenting journeys, 'one that requires imagination, revision, and plenty of faith.' This devotional is savory nourishment for the postpartum soul, beautifully accompanying the fresh fears, anxieties, frustrations, and tender epiphanies of those early years. I will be buying a copy of this timely book for all of the new moms in my life."—**Kelsi Folsom, poet, speaker, and author of *Breaking the Jar***

"Kim Knowle-Zeller and Erin Strybis are two women whose words come from hearts that are so for you and your mothering story. Reading these devotions felt like being handed a soft blanket and offered a place on their family room couch to rest. I'm thankful for their stories, their compassion, and their gentle invitation to truly experience God's love as you do the holy work of parenting."—**Katie Blackburn, contributing writer at *Coffee + Crumbs* and author of *Gluing the Cracks: Reflections on Motherhood, Disability, and Hope***

"Tender and true, *The Beauty of Motherhood* is a balm to mothers. Whatever moment you find yourself in on the sacred journey of motherhood, this book will leave you feeling seen, heard, and loved. Kim Knowle-Zeller and Erin Strybis kindly accompany us—the mamas—at 3:00 a.m., at the door of the daycare center, in the quiet of snuggles, in the center of unencumbered laughter, and in the middle of a tantrum (ours and our children's) as we build a life of love. With Bible verses, stories, practices, ponderings, and prayers, this generous and thoughtful book allows us to soften, take a breath, and rest in God's abundant grace. Motherhood is a remembering, a coming back home to our Creator's love for us all."—**Ellie Roscher, author of** *The Embodied Path: Telling the Story of Your Body for Healing and Wholeness* **and co-author of** *12 Tiny Things: Simple Ways to Live a More Intentional Life*

"Boy I wish I had this book when I was in the early years of parenting! I'm so glad it exists now. Kim Knowle-Zeller and Erin Strybis are great storytellers who have created well-rounded devotions that combine sweet moments with practical ideas and prayers. I know what I'm bringing to the baby showers in my future!"—**Melanie Dale, author of** *Calm the H*ck Down: How to Let Go and Lighten Up About Parenting*

"Finding the right devotional is like searching for a good, sturdy pair of shoes: you want it to hold up well as you journey through the mountains, valleys, and storms of life. This devotional is just that. Currently pregnant with my first child, I wholeheartedly trust Kim Knowle-Zeller and Erin Strybis's words to faithfully carry and guide me as I enter the adventure of motherhood. Becoming like those shoes that are well worn through the ages, this book will live on my nightstand for years to come."—**The Rev. Kelsey Beebe, founder of Dancing Pastor Ministries and host of the** *Lady Preacher Podcast*

"Being a mom is often incredibly hard, so I'm grateful for Erin Strybis and Kim Knowle-Zeller's words and stories and reflections that give a space for softness and gentle reminders that we are not alone in this calling of motherhood. Whether you are looking to weave your faith more deeply into parenting or need to borrow new practices and meaningful prayers, these pages will nourish you."—**Jenny Booth Potter, author of** *Doing Nothing Is No Longer an Option: One Woman's Journey into Everyday Antiracism*

"Like gentle, wise friends who know when you need an encouraging word—and dinner dropped off on your doorstep—Kimberly Knowle-Zeller and Erin Strybis offer mothers a lifeline with *The Beauty of Motherhood: Grace-Filled Devotions for the Early Years*. Drawing from their years of mothering babies, toddlers, and big kids, *The Beauty of Motherhood* brims with honest stories, peaceful prayers, and simple practices to nurture your faith in the joyful chaos of parenting. For every mother who's ever pleaded with God at 3:00 a.m. or wondered 'Am I the only one?' Strybis and Knowle-Zeller are here to remind us that we are never alone and God is always with us."—**Laura Kelly Fanucci, founder of Mothering Spirit and author of** *Everyday Sacrament: The Messy Grace of Parenting*

THE BEAUTY OF MOTHERHOOD

Grace-Filled Devotions for the Early Years

Kimberly Knowle-Zeller
& Erin Strybis

Morehouse Publishing
NEW YORK

Morehouse Publishing, 19 East 34th Street, New York, NY 10016

Morehouse Publishing is an imprint of Church Publishing Incorporated.

Cover design: Paul Soupiset
Typeset: Nord Compo

A record of this book is available from the Library of Congress

ISBN-13: 978-1-64065-600-0 (pbk.)
ISBN-13: 978-1-64065-601-7 (eBook)

For Charlotte, Isaac, Jack, and Adam

May you always know how loved you are.

CONTENTS

CHILDHOOD

INTRODUCTION

Six weeks after giving birth, I felt so depleted I didn't know what else to do but step outside and go for a walk. Our second son's arrival had shifted the very alchemy of our family, and though becoming a mother again overjoyed me, a small part of me missed the steadiness of life before. I hoped fresh air and movement would provide some semblance of normalcy. With my newborn wrapped against my chest and my C-section scar still healing, I retraced my favorite route.

Spring in Chicago is a tumultuous season. On any given day, you might see a downpour, light snow, or a rainbow arcing above the city. Any day could break you open with its bitterness and its beauty. On this particular day, the Windy City was living up to its nickname. As I took those first, shaky steps with my newborn, each gust cut against my jacket and invigorated my tired body. I'd been stuck in an endless cycle of feedings, diaper changes, and rocking, but breaking the loop reconnected me to the person I was before I got pregnant—a woman who loved to walk.

Much had changed since I last walked the neighborhood: the snow had thawed and left behind mottled brown leaves, green shoots spiraled out of flower beds, and a few crocuses were bursting from the hardened earth. Considering all the labor required to nurture creation, I felt a strange kinship with the One whose hands shaped the beauty I encountered. Taking in my surroundings anew, I walked. With one hand cradling my baby's head and another checking for his breathing, I walked.

But when I reached my turnaround point, I paused. My back ached from the weight of the baby, and I thought, perhaps I'd walked too far? My friend Kim taught me the African proverb, *When you pray, move your feet.* I've found the inverse is also true: *When I move my feet, I talk to God.* A prayer formed: *Help me, God. Give me strength to keep going.* Motherhood the second time around was just as sweet, if not sweeter than I remembered. At the same time, it demanded more endurance. To be needed so completely by my baby and oldest was a gift and challenge. Perhaps the heaviness I felt was the weight of everyone I was expected to care for—my newborn, my firstborn, my partner, myself? Perhaps my body was still healing.

The wind rose and kicked up some tree buds across the sidewalk. My breath slowed to match the rhythm of my baby's breathing. I recalled the many times I prayed for his health while pregnant. Adam was our rainbow baby, conceived a couple months after a devastating miscarriage. The day of his birth I cradled him close, cried tears of joy, and thanked God for our miracle. On the path, I felt my son's back rise and fall, and then it dawned on me: Adam was the answer to our prayers. He was evidence of God's goodness. I'd been so consumed with caring for him I'd forgotten the One who cares for me: God was with us. This truth steadied me, comforted me, and allowed me to take the next step toward home. Turning into the wind, I walked.

And this is what mothers do: we walk. We turn to the wind and put one foot in front of the other. We trust that we walk not alone, but surrounded by those who have mothered before us, those who mother now, and those who are to come. Sometimes we walk, sometimes we crawl, sometimes we chase after our children. Through it all, we believe that God goes with us, even when we struggle to see God. That's where Kim and I hope this book will meet you—in your hopes, doubts, wrestling, and trust.

This is a book for those of us making our way through the early years of motherhood. It's about heartaches and triumphs, messes and milestones, great fear and great joy. It's about motherhood as a journey, and faith as a journey, and the seasons we experience along the way—seasons of sleepless nights and baby giggles, temper tantrums and cuddles, growing up and letting go. It's about the moments we have and the feelings we share and the beauty in the ordinary. It's about the winds that threaten to throw us from the path and how we keep moving. It's about embracing God's grace in the midst of raising our children.

Grace is the way our kids fall asleep wrapped in our arms. Grace is the friend who shows up to feed us chili *and* rinse the dishes *and* hold the baby. Grace is offering and receiving forgiveness. Grace is catching the sunrise after another sleep-scarce night. Grace is waiting for you at the playground and in the school pickup line. Grace is witnessing first steps, first communions, first dance recitals. Grace is hearing our children murmur, "I love you, Mama."

Grace is in the bread and wine, the water and the Word, the prayers we pray, the hymns we sing. Grace is embodied by Jesus, who walked this earth just like us, who knew pain and suffering, awe, and delight. Grace is what keeps us going when motherhood feels heavy, when we cannot do one more thing, when we feel crushed by the stunning beauty of our children.

Whenever you open this book, we hope it reminds you that every little moment—every snack served, prayer said, and hug offered—is building a life of love. This book is less a roadmap and more a collection of stories, stories we know represent a sliver of the varied expressions of motherhood. We offer them with humility, knowing that we are continually learning about faith and mothering. We offer them, trusting in God who invites us to share our faith with others. We hope you'll pick up this book when you need a moment of peace between feedings, use it for group Bible study, pass it on to another mama who needs it. We pray our words help you see the beauty of this sacred calling. Beautiful things don't have to be perfect; indeed, what gives them their charm is often what's messy and raw. Spring wouldn't bear new life without the harshness of winter, and so it is with motherhood. In our wrestling to bear, raise, and love our children we are made new. We become mothers.

So let these words nurture you on your journey and point you back to a God who blesses you dearly—who's with you in the celebration and the grieving, in the laughter and the healing, who's whispering in every moment: *You are loved.*

A BLESSING
FOR BEGINNING

This blessing is for you—
the soon-to-be-mama,
the sleep-deprived, overwhelmed newborn mama,
the when-was-the-last-time-I-showered mama,
the joyful, grateful, adoring mama

the touched-out mama,
the cheering mama,
the depressed and feeling invisible mama

the mama serving purees and wiping sweet cheeks,
the mama delighting in her children's giggles and shrieks

the mama locked in the bathroom for a moment of calm,
the mama pacing hospital halls and praying the psalms

the mama Googling questions in the dark,
the mama sitting alone, watching her kids at the park

the mama at daycare drop-off who's holding back tears,
the mama waiting on milestones and wrestling with fears.

These devotions are for you—
so pull up a chair,
stretch your legs,
shed your phone,
and let down your hair.

The beauty of motherhood is yours
in this moment and stage,
in your worry, pride, love, and rage,
in cutting veggies and grapes,
in kissing cuts and scrapes,
in building Legos and blocks,
in playing with bubbles and chalk,
in rocking children to sleep,
in all the memories you keep.

Let these words remind you
as you grapple in faith
you're never alone,
you're drenched in God's grace.

The call to mother—
a challenge and a treasure
bestowing you with the name forever:
Mama.

INFANCY

LETTERS TO OUR CHILDREN
WRITING OUR STORIES

Kim

You search out my path and my lying down, and are acquainted with all my ways. Even before a word is on my tongue, O LORD, you know it completely.

—Psalm 139:3-4

stood in a local bookstore on the March day I confirmed my first pregnancy. My eyes rested on a paperback journal with a peacock feather adorning the cover. I touched my stomach and pictured the baby growing inside me. Wanting to mark this moment for my unborn daughter, I bought the journal.

Later, in the car, I pushed the seat back, allowing for more leg room. The day was warm enough to have my window open, which brought in a whiff of car exhaust and ensuing coughs. Holding my hand to my belly, I put the window up, but not before I smelled something else, too. Could it have been the beginning of new growth in the green leaves and crocus about to pop from the earth—the unseen beauty of new life just below the surface?

I rummaged in my purse for a pen and began writing.

Dear Baby Z,

It's real. We know you're real. It's official with a home pregnancy test and a doctor's confirmation test. Perhaps you're at 6 weeks. I had a feeling these last few weeks, but also didn't want to get my hopes up. I can't wait to see our story unfold.

Love,

Mama

Throughout the pregnancy and into my daughter, Charlotte's life, I wrote in this journal. Each word became a prayer for our life together, each sentence a way to mark the gift of being mother and daughter. Some days, I wrote the

5

events from an ordinary Tuesday. On others, I wrote from a deeper, more vulnerable place, like about the worry lodged in my heart.

From before time, God writes our stories into this world and knits us together in the womb. God knows our desires for children and our grief when our hopes are dashed. We pray, worry, and wonder if our bodies will carry a baby to term. We reach out to others. We swallow vitamins and exercise. We take one test after another. We cling to God's promises that God knows all of us—our desires and doubts, our body's quirks and beauty, our hope and joy. And it's this journey of knowing the love of God that I want to share with my children, and to remind them that God never leaves them.

The peacock journal bears witness to the truth of my love—a love that is grounded in God's love for me, too. Years from now, I want Charlotte to read my notes to her and feel love transcending the page. I desire my words to carry her when I'm not with her. I hope my words point to God's love for her and the world. I want her to know that her life matters—the mundane, the confusing, the heartbreaking, and the joyful.

Your child's life matters, too, and so does your life as a mother. Like the story I started on that day in the bookstore, a good story is being written for your motherhood.

PRACTICE

Write a letter to your child(ren) that you might read to them at bedtime or save for another time. Tell them about your day. Share the ordinary magic of being together. Write about what you notice and love about them. Let your words remind them of God's love written on their hearts.

PRAYER

God of love, you created me in love, and you know me inside and out. Thank you for your letters of love inscribed on my heart. Amen.

JOY IN A NEW CREATION
FIRST DOCTOR'S APPOINTMENT

Erin

Make a joyful noise to the LORD, all the earth.

—Psalm 100:1

Three days after giving birth to my second son Adam, I sat in the backseat of the car while my husband Jay drove us to Adam's first pediatrician appointment.

The sky was cloudless and the sun blazed brightly, giving each snow-stacked tree, roof, and sidewalk a hint of sparkle. Snug in my winter coat, I shifted my eyes to our newborn in his car seat. When I placed my hand on his chest to feel for breathing, his tiny fingers hooked around my index finger. My chest felt as if it might crack open. This snow, this baby, his mighty grip on me—it was almost too beautiful to bear.

Stopped at a red light, Jay turned around to ask how Adam was doing. Seeing the shine of tears on my cheeks, he changed course. "Hey babe, are you okay?"

I struggled to answer. "Honestly, I'm just so happy. I feel so lucky to have him," I said, blinking back more tears. "Maybe it's hormones... I think my milk's coming in. I just haven't felt this happy in a long time."

"Yeah, I get that," Jay replied. "I'm really happy, too." The light turned green and we moved forward again, turning onto the freeway.

After years of waiting for another baby and grieving a miscarriage, we received the answer to our prayers in Adam. I was overjoyed, but I felt strangely guilty about it, thinking of the struggles of others. While my family welcomed a newborn, joy seemed to be in short supply all around us, given the challenges of the ongoing COVID-19 pandemic. I thought of families I knew wrestling with loss and illness of all kinds. I considered the deep divides and power struggles in our nation and abroad. The weight of the world my children would inherit troubled me.

At the doctor's office, a nurse weighed Adam and measured his head. Then Jay stood by the exam table and spotted him while the pediatrician examined Adam's eyes, ears, and range of motion. Still recovering from surgery, I sat in the nearby chair and marveled at our tiny baby. Wasn't he in my stomach just a week ago?

When the pediatrician finished her work, she motioned to us to stay and chat with her. I cradled Adam and held his head against my chest. "Seems like he's doing great," the doctor said gently. "And how are you doing, mom?"

The tears arrived unbidden. "I don't know why I'm crying," I laughed, wiping off my cheeks with my free hand. "I'm well, really. I just can't believe he's doing so well."

Have you ever felt this way before? Like the blessings of your children are more beautiful than you can handle? Maybe you've wondered about their future, grasping for hope when you hear of terrible events near and far.

Attuning our hearts to the needs of our neighbors is a faithful response to an unjust world. While it's true that God calls us to love and serve our neighbors, God also invites us to "make a joyful noise" and celebrate the gifts we've been given. We don't have to choose between relishing joy and acknowledging hunger. We can hold the tension of both. We can hold onto hope knowing that God is on the move, active and working through creation to nourish God's people.

In a world hungry for goodness, joy sustains us. If anything, it's pure comfort food, meant to be savored.

On the ride home from the pediatrician, I sat beside Adam again and held his hand. His blue-gray eyes landed on mine for a moment, then fluttered shut as the car ride lulled him to rest. I closed my eyes too and offered a silent prayer to our Creator. I prayed for the people I knew who were suffering, and I gave thanks for newborn Adam. Then I let my tired body drift asleep.

PRACTICE

Find your ultrasound photos and share them with your family. Tell your child what it was like to see his or her first picture. Share what you saw then, and what you see today. Thank God for the blessing of new life, and tell your child about their Creator. Be bold and make a joyful noise. It is good to give thanks for the gifts we've been given.

PRAYER

Loving God,
thank you for this beautiful child.
I'm in awe of your handiwork.
May I fully savor the blessing of a baby,
trusting that, even in a hurting world,
goodness is mine to cherish
and mine to steward,
trusting that the advent of life
is evidence of your glory
to which I offer my thanks and praise
all the days of my life.
Amen.

Becoming a Mother
Seasons of Beginnings

Kim

"I am the Alpha and the Omega," says the LORD God, who is and who was and who is to come, the Almighty.

–Revelation 1:8

A day after delivering Charlotte, we hear a knock on the hospital door. "Photography," a quiet voice says, "Can we come in?" Attached to my breast, not even a day old, Charlotte's sucking. I cover up as much as I can with the white hospital blanket. Stephen, my husband, sits to my side wearing the same gray sweatshirt he slept in. HGTV Fixer Upper is on in the background.

"Come in," Stephen says, while I keep my gaze on our newborn daughter. Two awake, polished adults walk in, one carrying a notepad, the other a camera.

"Congratulations! We're the hospital photographers. We'd like to take your baby's picture." I see Charlotte suck a few times before completely closing her eyes. I glance at Stephen, who lifts his shoulders in a shrug. In the post-delivery fog and the newborn euphoria, I say, "Sure, we'll take photos." I want to capture this moment with our daughter as many new parents do. Yet, my body feels the exhaustion of the last hours. I want to remember her wrinkly fingers and brown hair, but I also haven't mastered nursing or changing a diaper. I want to capture her in all her newness and bring clarity to the fuzzy moments of becoming a mother.

I'm still wearing the hospital-issued nightgown. I haven't showered since before delivery. Stephen and I are mechanical in our movements as we maneuver Charlotte. Charlotte's eyes open abruptly as she's taken away from the comfort of my chest. She's lying at the foot of the bed wrapped in a green and white swaddle blanket with her hands fisted together near her face. Click after click, the photographer snaps pictures. With each photo, Charlotte's eyes remain open. Alert. Attentive. Aware of her surroundings. I believe she's issuing us a declaration: I am here. I see you.

I couldn't help but picture God bringing forth creation in all its beauty as I witnessed my own children's births. Those first few moments of awe at seeing my babies allowed me to wonder if perhaps in the act of creation God turned into the fullness of who God is. When reflecting on life before children, I've thought and heard other parents say, "I can't imagine my life before kids." It's as if in that moment, our worlds begin anew.

I wonder when we actually become mothers—is it with the desire to conceive, the first line of pink on the test, the hearing of the heartbeat, a first purchase of clothes, filling the baby registry, announcing to family and friends, in the delivery room, the first time holding our babies? Were we becoming mothers through all these moments and more in the slow accruing of an identity bound to another being, forever changing how we see the world? A mother's beginning is different for every woman, but in our becoming, what remains true is that each moment points us toward the God who is, who was, and who is to come.

We will never know or understand the fullness of God, yet the unknown doesn't keep me from searching for God's presence right here and right now. Holding each of my babies, skin to skin, in the breathing in and out of mother and baby, I could almost make out God's voice as if issuing me a declaration: "I am here. I see you. You are mine."

TO PONDER

When did you become a mother? Have you always wanted to have a child? Reflect on the small and big moments that thrust you into this new identity. Looking back, can you see God at work shaping you into the mother you are today?

PRAYER

Creating God, your Spirit breathed life into me, and you continue to bring forth new creations. You see me as beloved, and you have given me the name of mother. Draw me deeper into your love as I mother and tend to others. Amen.

Permission to Be New

Early Motherhood

Erin

And the one who was seated on the throne said, 'See, I am making all things new.'

—Revelations 21:5

When I open my front door, my whole body relaxes. My mother greets me with a hug and offers to hold two-week-old Jack. We sit on the couch and I watch her cradle my first son and smile sweetly. He looks peaceful in her arms. "How are you doing, Erin?" she asks, her voice tender.

"Mom, I had no idea being a mom was so hard," I confess, picking at my nails. "You were such a great mom. I feel like I'm failing."

"It *is* hard," she replies warmly, keeping her eyes on Jack. She looks up: "You're doing a great job, honey. Now go do something for yourself."

I thank her and retreat to the bathroom to shower. Hot water washes over my back and I reach for the body wash. This is the first shower I've taken in days. I want to believe her words that I'm doing well, but the list of struggles I'm facing seems insurmountable.

First there's breastfeeding, which I do every two hours, sometimes more, with gritted teeth because Jack's latch is too shallow. Dishes and laundry have been piling up too. And then there's my constant forgetting things—leaving cabinet doors open, misplacing my phone, overboiling the spaghetti—likely due to sleep deprivation. Did my mom ever feel like this? I think, turning off the shower.

After I'm cleaned up, I find my mom and take Jack to the rocking chair to feed him. I yelp when he latches, but the pain subsides after a couple minutes. When he's finished nursing, Jack spits up on my fresh clothes. "Time for an outfit change, buddy," I sigh, digging around in his dresser. I unearth a gray onesie and shimmy it over his torso. Across his chest are the words, "Hello! I'm new here."

The message makes me chuckle. Jack squints up at me with blue-gray eyes, and I think he's not the only newbie here. I'm new, too. I'd entered motherhood with the idea that I needed to master it, but I'd forgotten to give *myself* permission to be a beginner.

Now that my son is older, I've come to believe that early motherhood is a time of becoming. In those hazy postpartum days, we refashion our lives to care for our babies. Our familiar rhythms vanish, replaced by new schedules, new chores, new demands on our time. Armed with the knowledge we glean from blogs and baby books, we may feel a desire to "ace" mothering. Yet raising kids is less like solving an equation and more like crafting a story, one that requires imagination, revision, and plenty of faith.

In the book of Revelation, when God says, "See, I am making all things new" we can hold fast to those words and know they apply to us as we take on the title of "Mama." Day and night we summon power from inside ourselves to endure hard things we'd never faced before we had children. We do this because we've been transformed by motherhood.

When God created you, God gave you everything you need to raise your children. You don't need anything other than yourself. Trust God continues the work God began in your heart the day you accepted the call to mother. You are being made new.

TO PONDER

Where in your mothering journey are you a beginner? Where is God meeting you today?

PRAYER

Dear God, as I brave this new call of mothering, help me remember: you walk beside me, your love is certain, and you are making all things new—including me. Amen.

THE POWER OF NAMES
CHILDREN OF GOD

Kim

Jesus said to her, "Mary!" She turned and said to him in Hebrew, "Rabbouni!" (which means Teacher).

—John 20:16

Walking to school, a kid yells, "Hi, Charlotte!" from the backseat of a car waving to our family. A few more cars pass with waves and hellos. Charlotte runs ahead to greet other walkers. The principal and a handful of teachers stand at the entrance, opening and closing car doors, greeting kids by name. We reach the door. "Good morning, Charlotte," the adults cheer in unison. Even in our small town we don't know everyone at the school. Yet, they know our daughter and greet her by name.

It's a gift to be known by name and to have someone use that name and call us. When someone else calls my children by their names I'm grateful they took the time and attention to say, Charlotte and Isaac. Whether I'm at the store, pool, or walking around town, I love to hear their names in a myriad of voices from friends and neighbors.

Before our children were born, Stephen and I would make a running list of kids' names we liked. On long car rides we'd go back and forth on names we loved and names we could never use: names of family members we adored and names with negative connotations. For both children, we waited until their birth to know whether we were having a boy or a girl. That meant we had to have both boy and girl names chosen. I wish I could remember the precise moment we settled on our kids' names, or how our conversation happened. I only know that when I heard Charlotte and Isaac, I knew they were the names for our family.

The Christmas after my daughter was born, I received a note from one of my college professors. In response to our Christmas card with a photo of Charlotte from the hospital, she commented on Charlotte's gaze. In my daughter's eyes my professor believed she could see Charlotte choosing us as her parents. I looked again at the picture and imagined Charlotte knowing we were her parents even before she was born. I had placed so much emphasis on us becoming parents, choosing names, and preparing for the birth, I forgot, too, that Charlotte was also preparing to enter this world. Perhaps in some mysterious way, both parents and children are choosing one another.

Similarly, I believe our names connect us to the One who gave us our first name, Child of God. Our Creator chooses and names us. In your waking and sleeping, in your grief and joy, in entering and leaving this world, you, mama, are a loved child of God. That is your name first and foremost, and in the love that has claimed and called you, you are known. You have been chosen to live in such a time as this, mother to your children.

Another day the kids and I walk around town. Passing a backyard I hear, "Charlotte, Hi, Charlotte!" To our right stands a kid waiving. Charlotte waves back, "Hi, Matt!" The two know each other and delight in this chance encounter to be known and recognized by someone else.

Jesus calls to us, too. He knows us and delights in us. He meets us as we mother calling us by name in the voices of friends, family, neighbors, and co-workers, wherever we go.

Today, hear God calling to you and rest in that love. Remember your first name—beloved child of God.

PRACTICE

Use sticky notes or paper to write *I am a loved Child of God*. Place the notes on mirrors and at the front door of your home. Every time you see the words remember that God has called and named you.

PRAYER

Knowing God, you call me by name. You formed me and know everything about me. When others make me feel less than myself, help me trust that I am your beloved child. Every time I hear my name, may I remember your love and grace poured over me. Amen.

Swaddling Fear and Wonder
Managing Anxiety

Erin

> I will… put breath in you, and you shall live; and you shall know that I am the LORD.
>
> —Ezekiel 37:6b

At 11 p.m., I lie on the cold carpet next to newborn Jack's crib, watching for his breath. My own is bated. My mind hums: *Is he still breathing? Did he get enough milk tonight? How can I be so tired, yet wired? I should just go to sleep. I should just go.* But when I try to move, I cannot lift myself from the floor. Fear paralyzes me. I need to confirm my newborn's breathing.

Jack's life began with a lack of breath, a harrowing birth that required an emergency C-section and the removal of fluid from his lungs before he issued his first cry. He spent three days in the NICU, where I only held him for short spurts. This trauma is why I so often find myself here, next to his crib, or in my bedroom, pressing the baby monitor close to my eyes, checking for the gentle rhythms of his breathing.

Wrapped in a pale orange swaddle, Jack's chest rises and falls. I release the breath I didn't realize I was holding. Even though I am tired beyond belief, I stay watching him. His serenity draws my lips into a smile.

On the other side of my motherly worry is wonder. I marvel at the way my newborn's growing and changing. I see the world anew through his curious blue eyes. Simple things like early morning sunlight streaming into the living room or steam tendrils from a hot mug of coffee curling in the air hit differently. It's almost as if life pre-motherhood was a movie shot in black and white, and when Jack was born it snapped into vivid color.

From the nursery floor, I pray silently, *God, how did I miss this before? Your beautiful world. This gift of motherhood. Thank you for this child. For breath. Please keep him safe. Please release my worry. Watch over us tonight. And maybe grant me a little sleep? Amen.*

The soft buzz of the sound machine swallows the silence. My prayer provides a cocoon of comfort, so much so that I have regained the confidence to rise. I slip out and leave my swaddled son to dream.

PRACTICE

It is easy, as moms, to get caught up in the worries we have for our children. After all, we love them deeply and want them to be safe and happy. Take time today to make two lists, one for all your worries and one for all the wonders of your motherhood journey. Review them and see if you might share some of your answers with a trusted mom friend. When we learn we aren't alone in our concerns or joys, we cultivate deeper relationships. Let your conversation be a gateway toward prayer.

PRAYER

Inhale: God, you're in control.
Exhale: Release my worry.
Inhale: Thank you for the gift of my children.
Exhale: Wrap us in your steadfast love.

MY ALLELUIA SONG

BIRTH STORIES

Kim

So they went with haste and found Mary and Joseph, and the child lying in the manger. When they saw this, they made known what had been told them about this child; and all who heard it were amazed at what the shepherds told told them. But Mary treasured all these words and pondered them in her heart.

—Luke 2:16-19

Months before going into labor, I read other birth stories online, talked to seasoned mothers, and searched endlessly for different options for childbirth. The unknown mystery of bringing another life into the world filled me with awe and fear. *Would I be able to handle the pain? What if there was a medical emergency? What would it really feel like to deliver a baby? What if something went wrong?* I tried to remember that women had been delivering babies since the beginning of time and I was one mother in a long line of history.

I did successfully give birth—to one kid, then another. After both children were born, I wrote down their birth stories in journals. I wanted to remember the day and provide Charlotte and Isaac with an account of how they entered the world. Putting pen to paper weeks after their births, I wrote the tiny details of the conversation in the car to the hospital, the hours spent pacing the halls, and the nurses' kindness. I recorded the time they were born, along with how much they weighed. I included how many hours it took before I was able to push. I told them how it was their father who told me whether we had a boy or a girl.

The strength to bring a baby into the world is no small miracle. Our bodies are full of deep reserves of power, no matter how the baby is born. Whether you labored for hours, delivered in a hot tub, were rushed into surgery, felt every painful contraction, had your water break naturally, followed the birth plan, or needed medical intervention, your birth story is yours to remember.

Or if your child became a part of your family through adoption, the foster care system, or step relationships, your story matters and is yours to claim. You are a part of a long line of mothers.

I don't know if there's a technical term for the time between a baby's entrance into the world with their first cries of new life and the placing of the baby on the mother's chest, but in those minutes, there's such a rawness of life in all its beauty and messiness; a time where the baby feels the sting of cold air and no longer the warmth and security of the mother's womb. The moments of sheer relief for the mother. For me, that time, both seemingly forever and not long enough, could be summed up in a word: Alleluia.

Mary, too, knew what it was to bring a baby into the world. She held Jesus and heard his first cries. She drew him close to her body, feeling their hearts beat together. Jesus' life, a song of alleluia and hope for the world.

For all of us mothers, the sheer act of bringing new life into the world is an alleluia song—a prayer of hope in a world teeming with heartache and loss, an endless grace, and a love beyond all understanding. We are all God's song of hope and peace.

However your baby entered the world and became a part of your family, God sings a song of alleluia at every birth, for us and for our babies and for the world that we get to shape with our children.

PRACTICE

Have you written your child(ren)'s birth or adoption stories? If not, take time to remember the details from the day. If you've already written about your children's births, go back and read what you wrote, sharing with your children, and witness God's presence in bringing new life into the world.

PRAYER

God of all time, thank you for the mystery of birth. We come to you in our joy and our pain knowing that every child is knit together by you, our Creator and Redeemer. Our fingerprints and the hairs on our heads make us unique. Your grace in our lives brings us together as your people. Keep singing your song of hope for us. Amen.

Wonderfully Made
Body Image and Motherhood

Erin

I praise you, for I am fearfully and wonderfully made.

—Psalm 139:14

Days after giving birth, I assessed my body in the mirror. A woman I didn't recognize stared back at me, and honestly, her profile unmoored me. Her tummy was puffy and her ankles pooled out. Dark circles ringed her eyes and her hair looked ratty. Looking her up and down, I wished my old self, the one with the toned abs and easy smile, would reappear.

My lower body, with its C-section scar dotted by surgery tape, produced a mix of shock and awe. Shock at all the wear and tear, aches and pains, bleeding and bloating I experienced. Awe at what my body just endured, that I successfully ushered life into the world, with God's help. Yes, I had stitches and it hurt to sit, but I also had a beautiful baby to adore. Still, I wondered if my body would ever return to its prebaby state.

From childhood to adulthood, women receive complicated messages about our bodies. We're told we need to "bounce back" and lose weight after giving birth. We're told the only good bodies are those that mirror an idealized shape. We might believe our worth comes from our bodies, but that couldn't be farther from the truth.

Scripture tells us God created everything, including our bodies, and called it good. Mama, this is the truth: You are beloved just as you are. The body you have now is *good.*

When I am struggling with how I look, I recall the words of the psalmist, who praises God saying, "I am fearfully and wonderfully made." I remind myself that being wonderfully made doesn't hinge on my appearance, rather, it's about the marvelous things my body can do. This body has nourished and carried two children, raced triathlons, sung in concerts, worship, and musicals, embraced my spouse and children, balanced in crow pose, and served meals to my family. My body brings me delight.

What has your body done? Each scar, mark, and wrinkle tells a story. When women tell the truth about their bodies, we stop seeing them as objects to be admired and start comprehending their true potential—as gifts from God to be enjoyed. We can reclaim our changing bodies as evidence of a good God and a life well-lived.

A week after my moment with the mirror, I was rocking my six-week-old to sleep, trying desperately to convince him his crib was the best place to settle. I shushed. I swayed. I paced the room, head bent as I checked the droop of his eyelids. Then I peeked at my reflection and saw her—a woman with a softened stomach that had cradled her baby for 39 weeks, strong arms that nestled him close, bright eyes shining with love.

I'd been so tangled up in discontent, I nearly missed her: a mother.

PRACTICE

Take your body for a gentle walk, a massage, or a swim. Know that whatever shape your body is in today is a shape that's worthy of praise. Thank God for all your body can do and enjoy, a body uniquely created to mother your children.

PRAYER

Dear God,
when you knit me into my
mother's womb, you blessed
every aspect of my being and
called it good.
When you breathed life into
my lungs, I cried out,
and you saw that I was fed.
Help me remember:
I am not defined by
numbers on a scale,
my skin, my hair, the clothes I wear.

I am your gifted, beloved creation
I am a soul longing for connection
I am "fearfully and wonderfully made."
Amen.

Nourished

Community
and New Motherhood

Kim

A generous person will be enriched, and one who gives water will get water.

–Proverbs 11:25

ven before being discharged from the hospital following the birth of my second child, Isaac, I discovered my blood pressure increased. In the weeks leading to delivery at check-ups, the nurses had to double-check my pressure multiple times as the numbers kept getting higher and higher. I never needed additional medicine or a hospital stay, but the raised pressure was a new experience. Once Isaac entered the world, I assumed that my blood pressure would go back to a normal range. Postpartum preeclampsia didn't even register in my mind. So, when my blood pressure increased post delivery, I sat in shock and disbelief.

I can only describe the experience of having raised blood pressure as feeling "off." I could hardly focus. Baby and I both needed rest. During our first postpartum experience after the birth of our daughter, my mother cooked many of our meals. But this time around we needed more help. We were driving back and forth to the doctor for blood pressure checks. They told me to get rest and take my medication. All I could manage was feeding Isaac and taking deep breaths to try to lower my blood pressure. So, when our church young adult group started delivering meals for our entire family, I received their gifts with open hands. Their food nourished our bodies and our spirits.

I remember the lasagna and Texas Toast, the box of Panera scones, tater tot casserole loaded with cheese, chicken and Red Hot sauce, the homemade pizza, crusty and pepperoni-filled, and the garden vegetable soup. We found bags of ripe tomatoes, cucumbers, and fresh herbs on our porch. Iced coffee

23

and donuts were delivered for breakfast. Repeatedly I opened our front door to be met with warm food from our community. Each meal handed over felt like our friends were wrapping us in their arms and holding the wonder of this new child along with our fear and worry for health and healing. Their food became extensions of communion—a meal given and shared, a hope extended, and grace overflowing.

God nourished us through food and community and humbled me as a mother to receive the bounty of friendship and offerings before us. Sharing a meal brings us closer to others and to God. Jesus knew the power found in sharing a meal, and as mothers, we do, too. Throughout motherhood we find ourselves both receiving this nourishment and providing it for others. Maybe you have a go-to meal you make for families welcoming a baby, or perhaps every time you think of that fresh garden salad and homemade dressing, you are taken back to those early weeks with a newborn. You may know by heart that casserole recipe and with every chop of veggies and stirring of pasta, you offer a prayer for the family who will be fed.

Now that I've received these gifts of friendship and food, I try not to miss an opportunity to bring a meal to a home with a new baby, or friends in the midst of challenging circumstances. I've learned that it's not necessarily about what I bring—whether it's a takeout pizza and a bagged salad, or a homemade meal—but about how I show up: with open hands and food that declares you are not alone.

PRACTICE

Who in your neighborhood might need a meal? Are there neighborhoods or individuals outside of your local community who are facing food insecurity? Research organizations providing food and sign up to volunteer. Or, make a meal, a loaf of bread, or cookies for a neighbor in need and deliver them with a kind note. Remind God's people that they're not alone by feeding them both in body and spirit.

PRAYER

God of iced coffee and freshly made bread, you come to me in the form of friends and family. Your love tastes like spaghetti and meatballs. Your love smells like chocolate chip cookies. Your love feels like a hot mug of coffee. Your love looks like friends who don't say anything but bring a full meal to our table. Your love sounds like a doorbell. Open my hands and heart to receive your gifts, and when the time is ready, to extend them to others. Amen.

A WORTHY CALLING
GOING BACK TO WORK

Erin

However that may be, let each of you lead the life that the LORD has assigned, to which God called you.

–1 Corinthians 7:17

On my first day back after maternity leave, I sat in my car outside the office, crying. I had just dropped my three-month-old at daycare, but I couldn't bring myself to start my workday.

Jack hadn't shed a tear when I gingerly handed him to his new caretaker. She'd held him close and said, "Hiya, Jack!" then waved me out the door with a "See you soon, mom!" I walked out in a daze. After a year of togetherness—nine long months of pregnancy and three months of nursing, bonding, lullabies, and diaper changes—my baby and I were separated.

Looking in the rearview mirror, I wiped mascara streaks from my under eyes. *Will Jack be able to sleep? Will someone cuddle him when he cries? Why am I paying half my salary so strangers can care for my son?*

When I finally mustered the resolve to go inside, my workday passed quicker than I imagined. Kind colleagues left flowers on my desk and asked me questions about Jack. I had a backlog of emails to answer and fulfilling projects ahead but something—someone—was still missing.

I'd left my heart with my son at daycare.

In the days that followed, I wrestled with feelings of guilt. I loved being back at my job and I hated being separated from my baby. I worried that my working to support our family might adversely affect Jack.

A couple weeks later, my coworker sent me a calendar invite to a monthly moms' lunch. Sitting around the conference room were leaders from across our organization who'd walked the same path I was walking now. They'd juggled pumping in the lactation room and daycare pickups with meetings and deadlines. They knew the names, ages, and favorite activities of each other's children. When it was my turn to talk, they listened to my worries. They gave me the words of grace that I desperately needed to hear in that hard season: Working motherhood gets easier.

The more time I spent with them, the more confident I felt as a working mom. In that room, I saw *great* moms, moms who fiercely loved their children and their jobs. Moms who created miracles in the home and at the office. Moms who were using their God-given talents to help others. What's more, I was one of them.

Like the women in my moms' group, God's created you with a whole host of gifts for sharing with others. Whether you share them at home, in an office or in a variety of settings, you can trust that the work you do to support your family is not only good, it's holy. Contrary to what culture tells moms, your many and varied callings aren't in conflict with one another; they are part of the multifaceted, exciting, beautiful person God created you to be.

I'll be honest: Some days I wish I could have stayed home with Jack in the first year of his life.

While I can't get back the milestones and moments I've missed, I can cherish the ones I have, big and small—Jack's first wobbly steps from the coffee table to the couch; the curl of his lips whenever he's about to burst with laughter; summer weeknights spent sliding, swinging, and chasing the sunlight; the first time he called me "Mama."

Working motherhood, with all its challenges, has ultimately been a gift: it encourages me to pay attention to daily miracles with Jack, to thank God for him, to claim joy.

PRACTICE

Make a list of the work you do, both visible and invisible. How does that align with your interests and spiritual gifts? Where are you seeing room for better alignment? Can you make changes to your weekly rhythms to incorporate your passions? Is a bigger change needed? Lean into prayer as a tool for vocational discernment. Listen for the Spirit's voice when you are engaged in work that lights you up. Thank God for the opportunities to employ your talents in service to God and others.

PRAYER

Creator God,
You formed me with gifts to share
with my family and my neighbors.
May I know my work—in the home
and outside of it—matters.
May I answer each calling of the Spirit
freed from shame,
tethered to grace.
Amen

The Moon at 3 a.m.
Seasons of Sleeplessness

Kim

Yours is the day, yours also the night; you established the moon and the sun.

-Psalm 74:16

As mothers with babies, we know what it is to be awake at night. Over and over again, our babies need us to feed and change them. Some nights babies just don't want to sleep. I remember one particularly rough night of sleep with Charlotte. After days of disrupted sleep, my own tears fell in a cry of desperation, "Please, Charlotte, just go to sleep."

Around 3 a.m., I placed her in the car seat, pulled out of the garage, and drove our town streets. I passed an open garage where a group of men worked on a car, and some houses with lights glowing in windows. Otherwise, I felt like the only one awake with my daughter—who at least wasn't crying, but still had eyes wide awake. As I drove, I remembered my final night serving as a Peace Corps Volunteer in The Gambia. Sitting with the local women, one of the young girls turned to me. "You see this moon. It is the same moon that will shine on you when you're back home in the states. Look at the moon and remember us." Together we gazed up, mesmerized by the light. I studied the moon taking in its shape and contours, the way the light filled the African sky. The women seated with me had become family, and even though I'd be leaving, her words and the moon remained.

Driving with Charlotte that night, as I left town and entered the country, I saw the full, honey-colored moon. Rising above the corn fields, the same moon I saw in Africa shone before me on my rural Missouri country road.

In my moment of despair at the lack of sleep in our home, the moon reminded me that even in my sleeplessness, I wasn't alone. The same moon that covered my baby and I driving at 3 a.m. was the same moon watching over other parents. In houses, streets, states, and countries away, others were awake.

It's this same moon and the same God who whispers to you as you whisper to your babies: *I am with you.* This same moon shines for us all.

Seeing the moon drew me to remember not only God's creation and light, but others who were awake at this time. I thought about people who were sick or friends with a new medical diagnosis who might be awake worrying. I gave thanks for health care workers spending the night caring for patients. I remembered others with babies. As I continued to drive, my tears turned to prayers, and my frustration transformed to peace, as I gave thanks for all the people for whom the moon brought light.

Perhaps you're experiencing the moon at 3 a.m. You may know what it's like to walk your halls cuddling a newborn, or rocking your baby battling a fever, forging through a series of late-night cluster feedings, or waking to the screams of your toddler from a nightmare. The moon shines for you, too.

The moon offers light and hope to you in the darkness.

Under the light of the moon amidst a sleepless night, God speaks to us: *You are not alone, you are not alone, you are not alone.*

PRACTICE

Next time you're awake in the middle of the night, take the time to intentionally pray for others. Use your sleeplessness to connect to God by lifting up the names of people who need the reminder they are not alone. As you pray, remember the moon shines for all of you.

PRAYER

3 a.m.
again
awake
tears
screams
nighttime feeding
scrolling
tired
alone
until

I look
and see
the moon
shining
over me
for me
wrapping me in light.
Amen.

A Note to the Sleep-Deprived Mama

Longest Nights

Erin

> [God] will not let your foot be moved;
> [the One] who keeps you will not slumber.
> [the One] who keeps Israel
> will neither slumber nor sleep.
>
> —Psalm 121:3-4

Dear mama,

I see you rocking your baby to sleep in the middle of the night. Your sleep has been broken for months on end. You are so steeped in tiredness you're struggling to function.

And you're tired of people asking, "How's the baby sleeping?" The question seems unfair, like someone has dropped a bomb during a perfectly casual conversation—a judgment on your motherhood. The answer always feels too complex and too intimate to put to words.

You've read sleep books, or rather skimmed and dozed off reading them and used them as a pillow. You've heard of "cry it out" and co-sleeping from fellow mamas. You even got so desperate you hired an expensive sleep coach. Surely her rates meant she could solve your sleep dilemmas?

You have tried it all. But your baby still needs you to fall asleep, and sometimes you resent that.

I know this feels very hard. Like you are stumbling around in a cave, searching for a point of light, a sound, a breeze, anything to indicate a way out of the darkness. You know there's an exit, there has to be, and you feel and you feel around for it. But just when you think you've escaped, you find a dead end. The search for rest is maddening.

You probably don't want to hear any more advice, but here's what I wish I had heard when I was stumbling around in the dark cave of baby sleep issues: The only way out is through. Through the longest nights and even longer days. Through the transition from swaddle to sleep sack. Through the need for many night feedings to less and less. Through the shushing and tears to sweet, sweet slumber.

I know it's hard to believe, but one night your baby (and you) will sleep through without waking. It might be next week or another few months, but you can trust that you will find your way out of the cave. Sleep will come. Like smiling and crawling, sleeping through the night is a developmental milestone babies meet when they're ready. And all babies are different.

I have to warn you, that when your baby reaches this milestone, you may not be ready. Your baby may sleep through the night while you toss and turn, wondering if everything's okay.

You'll recall the hours you held your baby heart to heart, and the deliciousness of your babe falling asleep in your arms, wanting for nothing but you. You will miss the closeness you shared in your season of broken sleep. All that time you were cultivating your sacred bond, a love your baby will need in the seasons to come, a love that's still unfolding.

In the meantime, let God meet you in the dark.

No one knows the burden of the sleep deprived mama quite like our God who "neither slumbers nor sleeps," keeping watch over creation. What a comfort to know of our Creator's vigilance and care. What a gift to know that when we are feeling far from rested, God is with us—God still tends to us when we're most depleted.

The next time you are summoned by the cries of your tiny people, when you can barely keep your eyes open but you rise anyway, know that God is near, caring for you, too.

Know there are millions of parents across the world rising in the dark to soothe their children, a society of broken sleep.

PRACTICE

If you are currently a card-holding member of the society of broken sleep, you're in good company. Remind yourself of other moments in life when you were in the middle of a hard thing. What got you through? What do you need in order to make it through this moment, trusting that a day will come when you reach the light? Maybe a soothing weighted blanket, a hot shower, or an early bedtime. Be gentle with yourself.

PRAYER

God, meet me in the dark
and breathe life into these tired bones,
breathe life into me
and show yourself—
you are the light at the end of the tunnel
shining for me
leading me from heartache
to hope.
Help me see the beauty of the dark
to know you meet us in every waking moment.
Amen.

BLESSING OUR KIDS
FAITH FORMATION

Kim

Bless the LORD, O my soul, and all that is within me, bless his holy name.
Bless the LORD, O my soul, and do not forget all his benefits.

–Psalm 103:1-2

Every night, whether at home or traveling, I check on my kids after they've fallen asleep. Even though they are past the baby stage, I still use monitors. While they sleep, I say a prayer for their peace, their safety, and for God's love to envelope them. Our nighttime routine includes blessing one another as a family, but I believe you can never have enough blessings, so most nights I pray for and bless my children as they sleep.

Watching them through the monitor, fuzzy and gray-scale, I see Isaac's hands resting atop his head, a large dinosaur pillow to his right, and blankets and more stuffed animals surrounding him. Charlotte's blanket is askew with one arm and leg hanging off the bed. Through the monitor I say a blessing—*be with Charlotte and Isaac, Lord, give them rest and peace, keep them safe, and may they always know love, and be love for others.*

When I say a blessing over my children I don't say the words believing that they'll be protected for all time. I don't offer blessings to insulate them from harm. Rather, when we bless someone we offer tangible words to remind them they are not alone. A blessing is one way we can let others know that God is with them through whatever life holds.

We bless precisely because we know the world is messy, broken, and in need of hope and healing. We bless because God first called us beloved children. We offer blessings so that we can share light and grace in the world.

Every time I bless my children, I entrust them to God knowing that when hardship overcomes them, or when they've hit a wall with nowhere to turn, the words of blessings can come back to them and give them the courage to keep going.

We know we can't protect our children from everything. We know we can't keep violence and injustice from encroaching on their lives. But we keep blessing and proclaiming that goodness will prevail. As mothers we can use our voices to rally for justice and peace. As we bless others, we live boldly into the love and grace that God freely gives.

So this day, may you bless those you encounter and may you receive a blessing in return.

> The Lord bless you and keep you;
> the Lord make his face to shine upon you, and be gracious to you;
> the Lord lift up his countenance upon you, and give you peace.
>
> —Numbers 6:24-26

PRACTICE

Write a blessing for yourself and your children. What words of hope and comfort do you want them to know, and what words do you need to hear for yourself? Read your blessing over and over and remember that God is with you.

PRAYER

God, be with my children. May they feel love from the top of their heads to the tip of their toes and everywhere between. May they be surrounded by love in friends and neighbors. May they know what it means to be a friend, to forgive and be forgiven. Be with them in their sleeping and their waking for all their days. Amen.

EMBRACING FULLNESS
MOTHERHOOD AND IDENTITY

Erin

We have gifts that differ according to the grace given to us.

–Romans 12:6

take my first trip away from Jack when he's 14 months old. I'm flying from Chicago to Austin for a bachelorette party with my fabulous group of college girlfriends. Sitting on the plane, I keep having this creeping feeling that I've forgotten to pack something essential—my wallet, my phone, my hairbrush. I swirl my ginger ale and try to read the novel I've brought with me.

But my arms feel strangely empty.

Cold air blasts from the fan above me, and I pull my cardigan tight against my torso. High in the sky everything is quiet, apart from the static of the plane. I peer out the window. If Jack was here, he'd be nestled in my arms, the heat of his busy body warming me. I imagine the honeyed smell of his crown and the high-pitched peals of his laughter. I haven't forgotten anything; I just miss my baby.

I wonder what Jack's doing with his dad right now, and whether he's feeling happy. Will Jack cry at bedtime? Will Jay feel overwhelmed caring for him? Should I have left him?

Worries and guilt crowd my head and I try to push them out with thoughts of the impending celebration. I couldn't miss this trip for the world; I had to be there for my girlfriend. And yet, to be on this plane alone was like trying on an old pair of jeans I hadn't worn since getting pregnant. These jeans fit differently now, hugging and stretching in new places. Wearing them unearths a dozen memories of life before motherhood. I want to wear these jeans, but they feel uncomfortable. I'm not sure I can wear them well.

When I arrive at the home we're renting, I squeal and embrace my girlfriends. Even though it's been a decade since we graduated, we quickly fall into nonstop conversation. We share stories of our lives now, lives filled with children and careers and homes to tend. We explore the streets of Austin on foot and feast on fancy tacos. We clink palomas and take over the dance floor at the bar and laugh until our sides hurt. The trip is putting me in touch with the young woman I was before I became a mother, and I like her spirit. She's still inside of me, searching for room to breathe.

By the time I'm back on the flight home to Chicago, my body's buzzing with energy. I'm eager to hug Jack and Jay, but the part of me I'd let go dormant is awake and I don't want to lose her. How could I bring more of her into my life with my family? Stepping off the plane, I open my arms wide, ready to embrace the question.

Have you ever felt burdened by the myriad obligations that accompany mothering? Do you wonder if you'll ever feel like your younger self? Our lives are comprised of many different callings and God is with us in each one. God wants us to embrace the fullness of ourselves, including the parts that need to change and stretch. You're more than a mama, you're a child of God, a friend, a neighbor, a citizen, a person with dreams and talents.

TO PONDER

Who are you apart from your children? Make time for activities and relationships that put you in touch with your spiritual gifts beyond mothering.

PRAYER

God of grace, on days when I need a reminder that my identity is multifaceted, extending beyond the work of motherhood, grant me courage to seek out childcare and opportunities that reconnect me to the whole of who I am. Amen.

WAITING ON WORDS
SEASONS OF COMPARISON

Kim

The LORD passed before him, and proclaimed, "The LORD, the LORD, a God merciful and gracious, slow to anger, and abounding in steadfast love and faithfulness.

—Exodus 34:6

can't pinpoint the exact moment when I worried something might be wrong with Charlotte's speech.

As she approached her first birthday, I kept waiting for that first word. Every day seemed like the perfect day to hear her voice. At 18 months with no first word, our pediatrician recommended a speech consult.

We didn't know which story to believe: the doctor requesting a speech consult or the myriads of well-meaning family and friends who assured us she'd talk on her own time.

"Oh, she'll talk when she's ready."

"Our son/daughter/grandchild didn't talk until they were two, give it time."

"What do the timelines mean, anyway? Babies work on their own schedule."

A few more months passed and still Charlotte had no words. My worry grew in the silence.

As we approached her two-year well visit, we knew we had to address Charlotte's lack of words.

On my best days, I looked forward to the people who would guide us along this journey. On my worst days I spiraled into doubt and worry. If she can't talk now, will she ever?

When Charlotte was three years old, I counted on one hand how many words she could speak. Everywhere we went, I was confronted by other toddlers' words. At the playground, they yelled, "Watch me! Slide! Swing!" At story

39

time, they answered the librarian's questions about the animals they saw on the page. At the walking trail, they yelled, "Look, water!" At the kids' museum, they held a toy and yelled "Mine!"

While other children were rattling off stories and narrating their activities, my daughter laughed and cheered. While other children yelled for their moms and dads, Charlotte just lifted her arms, screamed with glee, and ran to us. With each passing day, I hoped we would hear a word or two from Charlotte. If only she started talking, then she wouldn't stop, I reasoned. I couldn't help but look at other children and see where Charlotte's words were falling short. I couldn't help but see my daughter and wonder what I could have done differently.

Comparison does that to us, doesn't it? Perhaps for you, you can't help comparing your home, feeding choices, kids' behavior, or screen time to others. We scroll social media and are bombarded with perfect images and Pinterest-worthy homes. It can feel like our lives will never be as good as others, and that our children will never catch up.

For so long, I only saw the things my daughter wasn't doing, not what she could do. While I ached to hear more words and sounds, I failed to see the gift in front of me: Charlotte caring for her dolls, her hugs, and how she flipped through picture books. I only heard the silence. In my worst moments I felt like I had failed. And I resented other parents who didn't have to worry about whether their children would talk.

During the months of waiting for Charlotte's words, I turned to God. I offered my pleas and cries, I shared my anger and worry. Releasing the fears and giving them to God allowed me to feel hope. Slowly, God invited me to offer myself compassion.

When I started down the road of compassion, I began listening for God's voice. *You are enough, you are loved, you're doing a great job.* God's faithfulness reminded me I wasn't alone and met me in the speech therapists who practiced one sound at a time with Charlotte and the other children who played with her when the words weren't there.

When I turned my attention away from what Charlotte wasn't doing, I opened my eyes and tuned my ears to the things that she could do. Yet, my doubts still exist. When we switched therapists I worried we'd lose momentum. The stories and words of other children still make me think Charlotte is behind in her language. I doubt and I believe, but all the while I keep my eyes open to God's faithfulness.

PRACTICE

Take time today to observe your child(ren). Don't compare them to milestones or to anyone else. Make note of how their eyes shine or the way their hair falls on their forehead. Listen to the cadence of their voice and watch how they run through your house. Give thanks to God in this moment for the children before you.

PRAYER

God of never-ending compassion, help me to give myself the same grace you offer me. When I doubt my parenting and spiral into worry, remind me over and over that you are with me, and that there is nothing beyond your reach. Amen.

FACING THE FULL SINK
GRAPPLING WITH MOM GUILT

Erin

And the peace of God, which surpasses all understanding, will guard your hearts and your minds in Christ Jesus.

–Philippians 4:7

pressed my palms into the lip of the sink and bowed my head. Empty bottles and breast pump parts sat in a pile at my right. To my left, a lime-colored bottle rack made to look like grass. A thought pulsed through my head: *Stop dawdling; it's getting late. Just start.*

I twisted the faucet to HOT and let the water run until steam rose in the sink and caressed my tired cheeks. I found the first bottle and twisted it open. A whiff of breast milk remnants invaded my nostrils.

Out came the dish soap. Then the bottle brush from my baby shower registry—a list created by a sparkly pregnant self I barely remembered. Now purple bags ringed my eyes—courtesy of 3 a.m. nursing sessions—and my hair was caked with dry shampoo after several skipped showers.

Earlier that day, when a colleague asked how I was doing with working motherhood, I chirped, "Great!"

How I really felt? Empty.

Just like this pile of bottles I have to get through before I can sleep. A sigh escaped my lips. I swirled dish soap in the bottle, rinsing it under scalding water. My hands deposited the clean bottle onto the artificial turf and reached for another. My mind was free to dwell on the scathing words my boss delivered earlier, chiding me for a minor accounting error. "You've been messing up a lot lately, it seems," she said, raising her eyebrows. She used the term "mom brain" to refer to me. Her words stung like a slap.

Swallowing hard, I reached for the cone-shaped pump part and continued my chore. I thought of my six-month-old's caretaker, who recently suggested, "Perhaps we ought to supplement your son's breast milk with formula?"

Pumping and nursing my son were something I could control when so much seemed to be spiraling. I felt like she was trying to take it all away. I could hardly breathe when she asked me. I refused her offer and vowed to increase my production.

Fat tears dropped onto the pump part. By now, I was sobbing over the faucet, tears mixing with hot water. I was failing at working and mothering. I was beyond exhausted. The pump part clunked to the bottom of the sink.

My palms found the lip of the sink again. One thing I could do was turn to God. To trust I wasn't alone. To ask for God's peace to pour over me. This time I bowed my head to pray. *God, could you just let me have this one thing? Let me feed my son. Please. I can't do it without you.* I also prayed for my boss, that she might have patience with me and see that I'm doing the best I can. When I opened my eyes, the empty bottles were still waiting for me. So were my problems back at work. But admitting my need to God brought a peace I couldn't fathom. The peace that my church's liturgy says, "surpasses all understanding." Peace to carry with me through the tough months of early working motherhood. Peace that flows from a well that's not my own—from the God whose love fills and sustains us.

PRACTICE

Have you ever heard the expression, "You can't pour from an empty well?" What would it look like to take time, even just five minutes at the kitchen sink, to fill your well with prayer? Take it a step further and find another mama to serve as your prayer pal. You could share your stories with each other weekly with the intention of praying for one another throughout the week.

PRAYER

God of life,
when I feel like I'm at the end of myself,
help me remember that I'm not alone.
When I feel as if I'm breaking under
the pressure of others' expectations,
teach me to pray.
When I feel as if I can't

live up to my own great expectations,
turn my heart to you for guidance.
You source the life-giving waters of nourishment.
Your love remains boundless like the ocean.
Now and always, may I quench my thirst
with your grace. Amen.

Prayers of the People
Embracing Worship

Kim

Rejoice always, pray without ceasing, give thanks in all circumstances, for this is the will of God in Christ Jesus for you.

—1 Thessalonians 5:16-18

n the early years of motherhood, I found myself sitting in the back of the sanctuary during Sunday worship. Whether one child was throwing a fit or one needed to nurse, sitting in the back allowed us to be present for worship, but also far enough from others to not cause a scene (and to be close enough to the bathrooms).

With my babies, I'd nurse while we cuddled. The sounds of the service—music, greetings, and prayers—comforted my children so that many times with a full belly, they'd fall asleep in my arms. Rocking back and forth in the rocking chair, with a baby nestled against me, I watched the congregation: up and down in the pews, listening to the stories of God's people, mothers coloring with children, fathers doling out snacks, teenagers fidgeting. All of it holy. All of it worship.

For fear of waking up the baby, many Sundays I'd remain rocking in the back instead of joining the liturgy. I wasn't able to get up and down and join the congregation. I didn't sing or speak too loudly. Yet, I learned in those early years of motherhood that this time in worship could all be prayer. My time in the rocking chair was indeed sacred.

I'd rock and pray: *thank you God, for this baby. Keep him safe. Give us all rest. May we all know love.*

I'd rock and pray: *thank you for this community and the voices joined as one in song. Thank you for the outstretched hands and the warm smiles. May we all grow together in God's love and grace.*

Sometimes I'd rock the baby sleeping in my arms, and I'd hear the prayers spoken by the assisting minister. Certain words would grab my attention, conjuring a whole host of new prayers. My attention turned to the world, and hope for healing, love, new life, and peace.

Looking at the congregation members in front of me, words bubbled to the surface.

Watching two children sleep on their parents' shoulders, I prayed: *May we all know such rest and comfort.*

Smiling at a high school couple surrounding one another with their loving arms, I prayed: *May we all have gentle hands to reach out to us.*

Witnessing a family bouncing twin boy toddlers on their knees, I prayed: *May we all be so deeply loved.*

Listening to the wind against the windows and watching the sun stream through the stained glass, I prayed: *Thank you for this creation and the abundance of beauty and new life. Help us steward this earth and preserve its bounty.*

Seeing the widow alone in the pew, I prayed: *Pour your presence on those who need a friend.*

Wondering about those who weren't among us, I prayed: *For those who would never enter a church, may we meet them where they are.*

The more I saw the people in front of me, the more prayers I had to offer. I rocked back and forth. My son slept. I prayed. Sometimes with words. Sometimes with sighs of gratitude.

I may not remember the Bible stories or the message from the pastor, but these prayers, I remember. This sleeping, this fidgeting, this tuning in and out of worship, this longing, this loving, this holding, this noticing, it's all worship. It's all prayer.

One breath and one rock at a time.

However you're praying—with words, sighs, or tears—God hears you. God hears the whispers of your heart and the screams from your gut. Wherever you are and however you feel, look around and see God's people inviting you to pray. For your life is a prayer.

These are our prayers. These are the prayers of the people. Amen.

TO PONDER

Reflect on your prayer life. Who taught you how to pray? Was prayer modeled for you growing up? How do you integrate prayer into your days with your children? If you would like to dig deeper into your prayer life as a family, consider choosing a daily prayer time during which you'll name people you'd like God to hold close.

PRAYER

Teach me to pray Lord,
with songs and sighs
with singing and dancing
with laughter and tears
with hope and heartache
and in all that I offer
may my life be a prayer.
Amen.

SOMEONE TO SEE ME
WORKING MOTHERHOOD/FRIENDSHIP

Erin

A friend loves at all times,
and kinsfolk are born to share adversity.

—Proverbs 17:17

M aybe she noticed my bloodshot eyes. Or heard me sigh as I shuf-
fled to and from the office lactation room. Something in my coun-
tenance must have told my colleague that I needed a pick-me-up
because on Tuesday morning she texted:

*I'm heading to Starbucks before work. What's your coffee order? Let me treat
you.*

After a long night with a teething baby, the offer was a godsend. From my
cubicle, I texted back excitedly:

You're amazing! Tall iced coffee with cream, please.

When my friend showed up to work, she slid the coffee across my desk
and plopped herself down in the chair across from me. "How's it going,
friend?" she asked.

"I'm exhausted," I said, shaking my head. "Jack had a rough night… and
I've got a lot of deadlines to meet today." I raised the coffee and took a sip.
"This helps. Thank you."

"Anytime, lady," she smiled, raising her coffee cup toward mine. "I see
how hard you're working. You're an awesome mom and colleague."

My eyes welled. Since returning to work after maternity leave, I'd felt like
I was walking a tightrope, straddling the weight of my work and motherhood.
Through the simple grace of a free coffee, my friend caught me when I was off
balance and teetering. She offered a steady gaze and dose of love to nudge me
closer to equanimity.

Isn't that what we all need? Friends to steady us when we feel a little
wobbly? Whether we're walking through those early, sleep-scarce nights of

the newborn phase or entering into a new season of behavioral challenges, or coping with multiple children and multiple demands, sometimes we just need affirmation that our efforts are enough. Sometimes we just need to see the face of Jesus in a friend to make it through. A little coffee doesn't hurt, either.

Whether you walk tall or wobbly, whether your load is light or your load is heavy, trust Jesus sees you in your mothering. Jesus sees you and calls you beloved and is there to offer you a dose of refreshment and encouragement. Keep your eyes open and look for the face of Jesus in the people who serve you. Look around for other moms who might feel a little wobbly, and be the face of Jesus to them, too.

PRACTICE

Is there a mom in your circle who needs a little extra encouragement? Reach out to her with an offer of a warm beverage and conversation. Let her know you've added her to your prayer list.

PRAYER

Dear God, when I walk wobbly,
steady me with your grace.
Show me the face of Jesus
in the eyes of my neighbors.
Help me offer that same care
to the people in my midst.
Amen.

Missing Puzzle Pieces
Marriage in Transition

Kim

Be kind to one another, tenderhearted, forgiving one another, as
God in Christ has forgiven you.

–Ephesians 4:32

A stack of puzzles sits atop our office desk. Each puzzle has at least one missing piece. We've searched couch cushions, rearranged furniture, and moved tables and dressers. We don't give up, at least not yet; the stack of puzzles attests to that fact. Their presence reminds us to keep looking, to keep hoping to find what is lost.

I want to tell my husband that our marriage, or our love more aptly, is like those missing puzzle pieces. Not necessarily lost for all time, but buried underneath layers of to-do's, meal plans, and playdates.

Does it feel like your relationship with your partner is on auto-pilot? You know the spark was there, but in the day-to-day realities of parenting, working, laundry, and dishes, it's hard to find energy for romance, or even an uninterrupted conversation. Do you feel like prioritizing time with your spouse comes only after all the things with your kids are done?

I try to remember the excitement and tingle of first love and the joy of being together on long car rides. I think back to late-night conversations and walks hand-in-hand. Those feelings are still there, yet most days I fear they're buried beneath the rigors and busyness of our day-to-day lives.

Some days I'll go to bed without saying goodnight or giving a good night kiss—not because I don't feel anything, but because I just can't do one more thing. Other days we'll pass knowing glances to one another, and some days our eyes hardly meet between food prep, laundry, work schedules, and shuttling the kids here and there.

My early love got covered up, buried beneath the daily piles of life with children and lost puzzle pieces under the couch.

The other day, Charlotte came running to us both. Cheering and exclaiming, "This, this, this!" as she showed us a puzzle piece. She placed it in the missing hole. The puzzle was complete once again.

She cheered. We cheered, too.

The piece wasn't lost; it was just waiting for us to find it. Waiting for us to be surprised by its presence once again.

There are moments when my feelings of love for my husband come bursting forth. I want to cheer, too, like my daughter. "This, this, this. This is the love I know and felt." I want to jump for joy again and fall into my husband's arms.

Do you know this joy at feeling once again what came with new love? Do you find it under piles of laundry, between text messages of who needs to be where, and over inside jokes at the dinner table? We want to look with awe at the life we've built and how far we've come. No longer young, but matured through the push and pull of raising a family, and growing into the people God created us to be, together.

I hope we'll keep unearthing this love, keep searching for it, for years to come. Leaving pieces of ourselves and this love wherever we go. We'll keep building and rebuilding; we'll listen to one another, we'll forgive and ask for forgiveness. Late at night we'll fall into one another's arms, resting, a perfect match.

We fit together, he and I.

We belong together like the one missing piece that can't be found until you've stopped looking for it, and find it suddenly right where you left it.

TO PONDER

Think back to the early days of your relationship with your partner. What drew you to them? Now make a list of all the ways you love your partner today. Give thanks to God for the maturing of your relationship and the steadfastness of love shown and given.

PRAYER

God of love,
today I pray for my partner

to remember them with love
to see our relationship
in all its beauty and contours
to recall that first spark
and to continue to nurture
our hearts in love
and keep turning to one another
fitting together
saying yes
over and over again.
Amen.

TODDLERHOOD

CRIES IN THE NIGHT
COPING WITH ILLNESS

Erin

But overhearing what they said, Jesus said to the leader of the synagogue, "Do not fear, only believe."

–Mark 5:36

At 10 p.m., the siren call of "MAH-mmy!" jostles me out of bed. I scoop my two-year-old up into my arms and ask, "What's wrong, buddy?" but Jack keeps on sobbing.

I take his temperature and see he has a fever. Holding him close, I squint in the half-lit bathroom and measure a dose of cherry Tylenol. After Jack slurps up the medicine, I rock him to sleep and put him in his crib.

Jack wakes again at midnight, then at 2 a.m., crying, "Owie, owie, owie—that hurts!" My arms cradle his body and we sway back and forth, back and forth in the darkness. *Jesus, take away his pain*, I pray silently. Then I add, *Mine too.*

I'm so exhausted, I'm on the verge of tears myself. I love my son with all my heart, but in moments like this, when his needs threaten to break me, another part of me wants to run away, back to a time when sleep came easy, and I didn't have to tend to a tiny human.

I think of a story about Jesus and Jairus from Mark 5. I imagine that Jairus, when confronted with his daughter's illness, knew my exhaustion well. So overcome was he with her pain that he dropped to his knees at Jesus' feet and begged for healing. Jesus responded with compassion, walking the weary father home, and even healing another unwell woman on the journey. When they arrived, the crowd discouraged Jesus from entering, believing Jairus should prepare for his daughter's funeral.

"Do not be afraid," Jesus assured Jairus. "Only believe." What happened next astonished everyone: the Healer took the child's hand in his and declared, "Little girl, get up!" And she rose.

When our children cry out in pain and we cry out in exhaustion, we can draw comfort in the knowledge that God always hears us. Healing is God's business, and whenever we care for unwell children, we model the One who makes everything new. In the same way you hold your children close, God holds you in a holy embrace.

After Jack's 2 a.m. waking, I do not place him in his crib. Instead, we stay in the rocking chair, heart-to-heart, and drift off to sleep.

Hours later I wake tangled in his limbs. A sliver of light pushes through my son's blackout curtains. Soon, I will call the pediatrician's office. For now, I hum the melody of "God Is So Good" into my son's ear, his fluttering eyelids and gentle sigh promise enough that miracles happen every day, and I can rest in this beauty, this small crack of light.

PRACTICE

Watching your child suffer from illness can feel almost as painful as experiencing illness yourself. To cultivate strength when you are weary: trace a heart or the sign of the cross in a safe place on your or your child's body, such as their back or forehead.

PRAYER

Healing God, when I feel as if my knees will buckle, when worries for my child's wellbeing threaten to drown me, when night waking becomes too much and I want to run and hide, make your presence known. You are the hands that heal, the light breaking through, the promise of dawn. You are the One who restores us to health. Amen.

"You're Doing Great, Mama!"

Seasons of Uncertainty

Kim

> We know that all things work together for good for those who love
> God, who are called according to his purpose.
>
> —Romans 8:28

sat on our teal-cushioned recliner, phone in hand, while newborn Charlotte nursed. We'd been up most of the night between feeding sessions, diaper changes, and learning the rhythms of this new world as mama and daughter. Exhaustion poured from my body. Doubt seeped into my bones. Doubting being a mom. Doubting my ability to care for another human. Doubting whether I was up to the task at hand. Doubting how I'd function on so little sleep. Doubting how my husband and I would ever find time for ourselves. Doubting my body would ever stop hurting. I was nervous about feeding my baby and whether she was getting enough food. I questioned everything from burping to swaddling to diaper changes. My phone lit up and I felt the vibration of a new text message. The words from a friend, also home with a newborn and a preschooler, couldn't have been more needed: *You're doing great, mama!*

Her words spoke truth into my weary body and heart: "You're doing great, mama."

How often have you been the mom in need of those four words? Do your days blur together so much you wonder where your own desires and dreams are anymore? Have you questioned or compared your choices for your children's food, school, and activities? When your patience is thin, do you rehash and regret harsh words spoken to your kids?

Hear me today: You're doing great, mama.

We're all doing great, mamas, because we love our children. We love them as we stumble down the hallway for another feeding, as we rock back and forth at 3 a.m. calming a colicky baby, and as we cut up grapes and make another peanut butter and jelly sandwich. We love them when we open our arms for a tear-filled hug, wash cuts and put Bluey bandages over knees, and while reading *Good Night Moon* for the hundredth time. We love our children even when the days are hard and we don't feel like we can give anymore. We love because we are mothers. We love because God first loved us.

If today you're feeling anything but loving, know this truth: You're doing great, mama.

If today you're questioning how you'll manage the to-do's, feedings, and getting a shower, know this truth: You're doing great, mama.

If today you're in need of a do-over from breaking up sibling fights and losing your patience, know this truth: You're doing great, mama.

In this season of raising young children, where the days are long and the doubts even longer, give yourself the grace to believe you're doing the best you can. And when you don't feel like you're doing great, remember God is always great and good. God has called you for this time and this purpose. God is with you.

Hear these words: You're doing great, mama. You are who you were created to be—full of love, grace, and infused with God's spirit. Rest in that love and God's call to you as mother to your children.

PRACTICE

Reach out to another mom with a text, card, or phone call. Remind them they're doing a great job. Tell them that you see them in all the beautiful ways they show up for their children every day.

PRAYER

God, my doubts and insecurities are nothing compared to your grace. Teach me to trust that you are with me and have called me to such a time as this. Grant me peace when I question my worth. Lead me to resting in your love. Speak over me the words I long to hear: "You're doing great." Amen.

MAKING HOME

COMPARISON
AND CONTENTMENT

Erin

But Martha was distracted by her many tasks; so she came to him and asked, "LORD, do you not care that my sister has left me to do all the work by myself? Tell her then to help me." But the LORD answered her, "Martha, Martha, you are worried and distracted by many things; there is need of only one thing. Mary has chosen the better part, which will not be taken away from her."

–Luke 10:40-42

A wall of pink ceramic tile first laid in the 1940s frames our shower, except for one spot covered in plastic. The plastic was a temporary fix after a tile broke; however, it's been there so long, my children don't notice it. But I do. Whenever it's bath time, I'll stare down at the missing tile and think, "We really ought to replace that."

At a recent playdate, my mom friends share similar woes. One bemoans her overgrown backyard, and the other laments stacks of laundry piled high in her living room. I nod empathetically, considering the laundry languishing in my bedroom and the weeds in our flowerbeds.

My friend Brigit holds her daughter in one arm and pushes her son with her other. "No matter what," she says, pushing the swing a little harder, "Something always gets the short shrift." She means the tension between caring for our homes and our children.

I roll my baby stroller forward and backward, wondering why moms feel so much shame about the state of our homes. Somewhere along the way, we learned houses and yards were the adult version of report cards. Who teaches us this? Is it our parents? The media? And why is it so hard to keep up with all the housework? I thought that, by my thirties, I'd have everything more put together. Honestly, I often feel like I'm barely passing.

I used to think my home was messy because I worked full-time. I thought moms who stayed home were better than me at managing the never-ending piles of dishes and laundry. Now that I'm staying home, I know that the mess has less to do with where I work and more to do with the fact that keeping your home clean with kids underfoot is as impossible as stopping a dandelion puff from scattering seeds.

My complicated feelings about my home bring to mind the story of Martha, Mary, and Jesus. When Jesus comes to visit them, Martha busies herself with many tasks, likely preparing food and setting the table. Meanwhile her sister Mary keeps talking and talking with their guest; she is far too distracted to take on any of the housework, at least, in Martha's eyes. When Martha complains about her sister's laziness, what Jesus says next surprises her:

"Martha, Martha, you are worried and distracted by many things; there is need of only one thing. Mary has chosen the better part, which will not be taken away from her."

While some interpretations of this tale pit the two sisters against each other, the way I see it, Jesus wasn't suggesting Martha's work didn't matter, rather, he could see how much Martha was carrying, and he wanted to give her permission to release some of her work. He longed not for the perfect hostess, but for her company. The same remains true today: Jesus wants to spend time with us.

Back at the playground, Jill weighs in on the conversation while playing catch with her preschooler. "I have grandparents living on either side of me. Their lawns are always immaculate," she says, chuckling. "But they tell me they'd trade it all in a heartbeat to have little ones underfoot again." Her words land like a hug I didn't know I needed.

At bath time, I fill the tub with bubbles and scrub my boys' bodies with care. My oldest son giggles and serves me cups full of foam, claiming they're coffee. The baby kicks his legs and squeals as I sprinkle him with water. I take a washcloth and swirl it gently against the crown of his head. When their baths are done, I wrap the boys in fluffy bath towels, kissing each of them on their foreheads. When my sons are older, will they remember the tiled walls or the way they felt splashing in the tub?

So, there's a missing tile behind our shower curtain. But if Jesus were to visit today, I doubt he'd care about it. Neither do my kids. A home doesn't have to look perfect to be holy. And I don't need to fix anything to offer them my presence.

TO PONDER

What's your version of the missing tile? Imagine that spot in your house and see if you can reframe it as a sign of love for your family.

PRAYER

Dear Jesus, sometimes I get so consumed with all that remains undone at home that I lose sight of my own worth. I think that these home flaws and unfinished chores mean I'm failing as a mother. Help me remember my worth comes not from work, but from my identity as God's child. And when my to-do list threatens to overwhelm me, guide my heart to what matters most to you—a relationship with you and with my family. Amen.

Each Day a Gift
Days of Small Things

Kim

This is the day that the LORD has made; let us rejoice and be glad in it.

–Psalm 118:24

On top of my dresser between pictures of the kids, ChapStick and earrings, a small rectangular book sits with a colored pen next to it. The book's location and the words on the cover—*One Line A Day*—remind me to stop and pause each night. For seven years, I've been coming to this dresser to write about my days in only a few lines.

I grab my favorite purple pen and start writing. I only have a few lines to tell about my day and what we all did: the food we ate, the places we visited, the times of reading books on the couch, playtime at the park, and our walks around town.

I started my five-year journal when Charlotte was two, as a new way to mark and honor the days. At the time, our life was filled with playdates with friends, naps, books, and church. A few weeks into writing, I found out I was pregnant again. And from then on, the journal became a time capsule of our family of four, the simple, beautiful, and hard stories of our lives, captured with a few sentences every day.

For the last seven years, we've lived in the same town with the same people, and we worship at the same church. Yet, each line I write represents the growth and experiences that are transforming and enriching our lives. When I write about the kids playing at the playground, I can see their growth by their willingness to slide down the slide or climb across the monkey bars. Our times with books on the couch are changing, as Charlotte takes her turn reading to us. Our memories in the kitchen not only include the food and baked goods we've made but the times the kids have helped mix, pour, and bake for others. Each night as I write and remember our days, I realize I'm praying.

Prayers of gratitude for wet kisses and small hands, reciting the alphabet and hearing stories come to life, walks around town and phone calls with family and friends. Prayers of being fed and feeding others, fresh baked bread and homemade meals shared, laughter and meltdowns around the table. Each day a gift.

When I read through the days turning into years, I see one word more often than others: good.

After all the long nights feeding the baby, the meltdowns over what clothes the toddler would wear, the endless pile of dishes, the worry about a family member's recent diagnosis, the food to be cooked, the distractions, the constant busyness, and the coordinating of schedules, the days are good.

Some days you may wonder how the hours passed and think about what you accomplished. It feels easier to think about what went left undone and when the kids couldn't get along or where you lost your patience. When you can't remember the last shower, and step on Legos again, and reheat your coffee for the fifth time, the days blur together.

Yet, as night comes and I'm ready for bed, the words come naturally.

A good day.

I lived. I loved. I prayed. I played. I wrote. I read. I messed up. I asked for forgiveness. I stumbled. I forgave. I yelled. I lost my patience. I rested.

Every night I come to the dresser and open my journal and am able to see the day for what it is—a gift to experience in this one, precious and fleeting life.

This life is your gift, too. Ready for you in all the ordinary and mundane glory. Open to you in mismatched socks, snacks for dinner, and moments watching the clock tick by. Each day a gift waiting for you to experience. Thanks be to God.

PRACTICE

This week, take a few minutes at night to write a couple lines about your day. Give thanks to God for the gift of the life in front of you, the one you're living, the one full of grace.

PRAYER

Dear God, help me to see you in my days. In every meal prepared, in breaking up fights, in emails and to-do's, in taking out the trash, in registering for activities, keep my eyes attentive to the gifts before me. May I know deep down the beauty right here, right now. Amen.

FORGIVENESS AT MEALTIME
MANAGING EMOTIONS
AND SAYING SORRY

Erin

The LORD is merciful and gracious,
slow to anger and abounding in steadfast love.

–Psalm 103:8

made my toddler his avocado toast exactly how he wanted: toast—medium burnt, avocado—smashed but not smooth, topping—a mix of salt and cayenne pepper. I placed it in front of him and said, "Jack, here's your breakfast."

My son took one look at his toast and stuck up his nose.

"Jack, what's wrong?"

"Too much spicy," he declared, pushing his plate away.

"But it's what you asked for, honey," I pleaded. "I thought you liked spicy?"

"No spicy!"

"Alright," I sighed. "I'll eat this one and start a fresh one for you."

I put another piece of toast into the toaster. I smashed another quarter of avocado and sprinkled it with salt only. I sliced it diagonally and placed it in front of Jack again. Then I glanced at the clock. We needed to get moving if I was going to make it to work in time.

Jack took a nibble of the toast and scrunched up his face. "No toast."

"Jack, this is exactly what you asked for…" I said, gritting my teeth. If my life was a cartoon character, this was the point in the story where my face boiled red. Something animal-like surfaced inside of me. How could he refuse the new toast MADE EXACTLY HOW HE WANTED IT?!

My fist smashed the toast. Immediately my cheeks flushed bright with embarrassment and shame. What was I doing? I looked at my toddler. Jack's eyes were wide with alarm. Bits of avocado had sailed through the air and landed all over him. Then I touched my face and felt the slime of avocado and released a tiny chuckle. Hysteria took hold and I couldn't stop laughing. Jack, confused, began laughing, too.

We all have moments in motherhood when rage rises to the surface: kids who won't go to bed, incessant whining, the struggle to get out the door in the morning. When we feel anger at our kids, it might surprise us with its intensity. What do we do with it? And what do we do when our emotions cause us to falter?

Our God is a God of grace and redemption. We can lean on God in these hard moments and remember that Jesus encourages us to confess our sins and ask for forgiveness. We own up to our mistakes and make things right. God doesn't ask us to be perfect. And our kids don't need a perfect mom, either. They need a mom who shows them they can mess up, receive God's grace and try again the next day, trusting that God will be there to guide us in a right relationship with others.

I took my fingers and wiped a bit of avocado from my son's cheek. "I'm so sorry, honey," I said. "Mommy messed up when she got really mad."

Jack laughed and cupped my cheeks with his messy fingers. "Silly Mommy," he said.

"Silly Mommy," I repeated. "Now let's get you cleaned up and try again for another breakfast."

TO PONDER

Where in your motherhood life do you need to seek forgiveness? Tell God what's on your heart, trusting God already knows. God waits for you with open arms, ready to embrace you in love and forgiveness.

PRAYER

God of big feelings and little people,
God of tiny whims and large frustrations,
when I get it wrong, grant me
a voice quick to apologize,
a heart eager to repair,

a spirit committed to repentance.
Guide me with your perfect love
and immerse me in grace
all the days of this mothering journey.
Amen.

GOD'S FAVORITE

SEASONS OF TRUST

Kim

See what love the Father has given us, that we should be called
children of God; and that is what we are.

—1 John 3:1

Every night we ask our kids to share their favorite part of the day. It helps
us give thanks for the small, yet meaningful ways God's presence breaks
through in our lives. This practice allows us to look back on our time
with gratitude. When many of our days seem to be on repeat, or full of worry,
challenges, and uncertainty, it is powerful to take a moment of reflection and
say, *"God, we know you were here today. Thank you. Thank you for showing up
in books, blocks, meals, and walks around town. Thank you for being with us
in meetings, worship, and answering emails. Thank you for showing up in our
family."*

On the nights I get Isaac ready for sleep, we sit in his bed with his body
cascading over me, almost too big to be held. We settle into the warmth of
construction site sheets and stuffed animals surrounding us. I hold my son and
feel held by the bed.

I ask him again, "What was your favorite part?"

He looks up at me with his pointer finger directed at me.

I never tire of seeing his response—his pointing to me. I am his favorite
part of the day.

There are days when I yell and lose my patience. There are days I focus
on everything else *but* my children. There are days I doubt my faith and God's
presence. But when I watch Isaac I see that he is not concerned about any of
that. You may feel this challenge, too, and wonder if God's love could find you
in your doubt and uncertainty, and in the day-to-day rigors of raising children.
Our children know innately that they are loved. They know their parents love
them. They trust our love will never leave.

So it is with God.

The maker of heaven and earth claims us as beloved children, people to comfort, rock, and hold close. If we could ask God to share with us what God's favorite part of the day would be, I imagine *we* would be the answer. God watches us raise our children as best we can and offers new mercies every day. God sees the intricacies of our hearts, knows the number of hairs on our heads, understands our thoughts, sees our wrongdoings and missteps, yet our Creator never stops loving us. Today, remember that you are seen and you are God's favorite part of the day.

TO PONDER

What would it look like for you to believe you are God's favorite part of the day? Especially on days that are hard, remember that you are created in love. Look back on your day and picture God holding you and rejoicing in you, giving thanks for the beauty that is you.

PRAYER

Thank you for the gift of today.
In my rising, help me to see you.
In my breathing, help me to feel you.
In my movement, help me to trust you.
In my resting, help me to find peace.
Amen.

EVERY ENDING A BEGINNING
MILESTONE: WEANING

Erin

> But I have calmed and quieted my soul,
> like a weaned child with its mother;
> my soul is like the weaned child that is with me.
>
> —Psalm 131:2

When Jack was 17 months old, we decided to wean him. He only nursed for comfort at the head and tail of the day, but lately, those sessions had disrupted his sleep patterns, and we knew something had to change. Jay handled the transition while I traveled to Boston for a three-day work project.

The night I returned, I cradled Jack at the foot of his crib and sang a lullaby. He craned his head toward my chest. "Milk? Milk?" he asked sweetly. My stomach dropped.

"Mommy doesn't have any milk now," I whispered, pulling him into a hug. "I'm sorry, buddy."

"Milk?" Jack repeated. I shook my head "no" and placed him in his crib ever-so-gently. He screamed. Panic rose in my chest. I scooped him back up. This time, Jack's cries turned to howls and soon I was crying too—big, fat tears. My mind reeled: *Look what you've done. Will your son ever forgive you?*

"Erin, Erin, are you okay?" my husband's voice broke through the noise; it was coming from the kitchen.

"No," I blurted, wrestling our wild toddler from head-butting me. "Haaalp!"

Shortly thereafter, I felt my husband's arms around my waist while I clung to our son. "Shhh, shhhh," he shushed, pecking me on the cheek and moving us side-to-side in a kind of slow dance. Our wails became whimpers. Our tense bodies softened. The three of us swayed until Jack relented and fell asleep.

Later that night, I stared at the darkened ceiling while attempting to sleep. I loved everything about breastfeeding my son: the soothing effect it had on him, the bond it created, the feel-good chemicals it released. Now our special time had ended. I wept and wondered silently: *What would ever replace it?*

In the days that followed, I felt so low I struggled to get out of bed in the morning. Nights were worse: Jack refused to be rocked to sleep at bedtime. He screamed, shouted, hollered, kicked. His resistance made me feel even more guilty. Some nights I cried, but sometimes I felt angry. Once, I grew so mad I stalked out of Jack's room and fumed to Jay, "I can't go back in there—*you* handle him."

Back in our bedroom, I held my phone to my face and Googled "weaning and depression." A handful of articles popped up. I read all of them. The deep heartache I'd felt? I discovered it was common and could be connected to hormonal fluctuations. Once I knew I wasn't alone in my big emotions, I allowed myself to mourn this milestone without shame. With time, the grief lifted.

In my short journey as a mom, weaning was one of the hardest milestones I've encountered. If I could speak words of love over my younger self during that season, I'd tell her:

You did it, mama. You breastfed your son for 17 months—that is something to celebrate! Allow yourself to grieve without guilt. Your pain and loss are real. But also? Look out for hope. Look for God in the people who lift you up when you feel as though you could buckle. Look for new opportunities to bond with your child—watching Sesame Street, *taking walks, sculpting Play-Doh. One day, you'll look around and see your relationship with your son transformed and refined. Likewise, you'll discover newfound free time for activities that light you up—writing, yoga, and cooking. Mama, weaning is one of myriad endings you'll encounter on the road of motherhood. And with every ending, God offers us a new beginning. Seize yours.*

TO PONDER

Children grow so quickly—from exclusive breastfeeding to fruit and veggie purees to table foods to weaning, from crawling to toddling to walking to full-out running, from cooing to babbling to words to phrases. Sometimes the change hits especially hard. What hard endings have surprised you? Where did grace show up in the midst of it?

PRAYER

Mothering God,
you know what it means to live in the tension
of need and independence.
When change with my child hits hard
grant me
ears to hear your voice,
eyes to see your face,
hands to feel your touch,
embodied in the grace
that surrounds me.
Amen.

GROWING UP AT THE PARK
SEASONS OF LETTING GO

Kim

You water its furrows abundantly, settling its ridges, softening it with showers, and blessing its growth.

—Psalm 65:10

From our living room, we look out a large window past hanging baskets and see the town park. In the summer, large green oak leaves make a canopy over the playground set: two yellow slides, a tire swing, and a cement tunnel. The red paint is chipped after so many hands and feet have made their mark. Often, I hear children laugh with glee, the creak of the tire swing, and the groan of wooden planks.

Charlotte is seven months old the first time she swings. We slide her into the bucket seat and make sure not to bunch her legs in the openings. We keep checking for any sign of fear. Stephen moves to her back and gently pushes her while I stand ready with my camera to document this moment.

A smile forms on her face. "You're swinging, baby girl!" I cheer as I witness this first moment of joy, the beginning of learning to let go.

By the time Charlotte is four and Isaac is a toddler, I sit on the bench watching Charlotte as she runs up and down the slide, crawls on the ladders, and pumps her legs on the swing. That is, until almost two-year-old Isaac runs to the ladder to place his hands on the bar and looks up. I run behind him, with my hands outstretched, and watch him lift one foot up on the rung. He turns over his shoulder and gives me a smile. He's not even two yet and wants to climb up the ladder. By himself.

"Up top!" He tells me with a grin. I remain close to him, both hands ready to catch him.

I coach him. "Put one hand up and then the other. Good job. Now your feet. One up and then the other foot." Suddenly Charlotte's beside him racing him to the top. "Bubba climbing up, Momma!" As if I needed the reminder.

73

At the last step he pulls himself to a crawl and arrives on the platform. Plopping down he turns to me with a smile as big as his face, his bright blue eyes shine and he says, "up top!"

"Yes, good job, Isaac!" I say, as I turn to take myself back down the ladder, one step at a time. I think about how I'll need to let go all over again.

Lots of times I'd like to do things for my children: lift them up, push them forward, spot them while they flip upside down. But mostly they want me to watch them and to learn to do that thing on their own.

At the park, I'm not the one physically exerting myself climbing and sliding, but my mental energy goes to holding myself back and letting the learning unfold. I want to jump up if their foot slips and I want to hold their hand across the top of the jungle gym. But I stop myself and watch and continue to offer my encouragement.

That's when I see the growth in me, too, and my ability to let my kids learn on their own. The learning in motherhood never ends, for us and for our children. Many mothers know the push and pull of wanting to help their children, but also desiring they figure it out on their own. Whether it's in relationships with others, putting together a puzzle that feels impossible, making food, or doing school work, the gift comes in learning to be near them in support and encouragement, but watching them take flight. And this is where transformation happens—for our kids in their strength, resilience, and growth, and for us, in learning to trust that the way forward is paved with mercy and grace.

TO PONDER

What place or space in your community have you witnessed the growth of your child(ren)? Ask your kids what memories they have from that place. Take time to recount those memories and where you've watched change in yourself and your kids. In the transformation, give thanks that God is with you.

PRAYER

Dear God, thank you for these children and their growth. Every day they astound me. Every day something new is emerging. Strengthen my heart to bear witness to this growth trusting you are with them. May peace wash over me as they are drawn deeper into your world and make their way on their own. Amen.

WHAT WE CARRY
EMOTIONAL LABOR

Erin

Take my yoke upon you, and learn from me; for I am gentle and humble in heart, and you will find rest for your souls.

—Matthew 11:29

As a teenager, I spent hours poring over *Glamour*. One of my favorite features displayed the contents of a real woman's purse. Each item was carefully curated—a bold shade of lipstick, a stylish wallet, bobby pins, and perfumed hand lotion. I loved imagining what essentials I'd put in my purse when I grew up and had more money to burn.

Today both the look and contents of my bag would likely make my teenage self chuckle. Diapers. Peach-tinted lip gloss. Baby wipes. Crayons. Silly putty. Insurance cards. Backup pacifier. One granola bar, half-eaten. Two nursing covers, wrinkled. Crumbs. Car keys. Sanitizer. Tissue.

And those are just the tangible things!

If someone created a magazine feature for my body, mind, and soul, you'd learn I carry:

Fear. Mom guilt. Anxiety. Worry. Extra baby weight. An actual baby. Eye crinkles. Laugh lines. A running tally of groceries needed, chores half-finished, play dates to plan, appointments to make, emails to be written.

And so many questions: *Did I handle that well? Will my kid be OK? Could this be a possible case of [diagnosis]? Will I ever sleep well again?*

Sometimes, the heaviness of it all sinks into my shoulders and lingers. I lie awake at night and toss and turn while the questions churn and my body tenses, a warning that I am close to buckling.

The truth is, I want to be free. I don't want to keep second-guessing how I parent. All this worry I've been conditioned to carry? I would gladly shed it. (I don't love carrying diapers and wipes either, but someday soon I'll carry a smaller bag.)

75

If I could craft another feature on what I carry, I'd take a picture of my open hands. Open hands remind me of hiking with my parents when I was a preschooler. My mom used to give me a little baggie to fill with flowers, rocks, and leaves. I loved collecting these tiny artifacts as we walked. Inevitably, we'd reach a point when I'd peter out and groan, "Daaaad, my legs are stuck together!" He'd hoist me onto his shoulders, and I'd ride high and carefree for the rest of our walk. I don't remember what happened to my baggie, but I do recall my hands clinging to my father. The image reminds me that—in every worry I'm clutching and in every aspect of control I grasp for—God is there, carrying *me* through.

In the same way we carry our children's things for them, God can carry our doubts and worries, freeing up space for more: Laughter. Silliness. Hope. Awe. Love.

PRACTICE

In your home, do you serve as the primary family manager, or do you split up tasks with your partner evenly? Is there anything you could use help with—if so, can you ask your family or friends for extra support?

What burdens can you lay down at the feet of Jesus? What worries can you share that come from your metaphorical bag? Remember: God can sit with you in the unknown—you don't have to do the heavy lifting of love alone.

PRAYER

Dear God, on the days everything I carry feels as if it could crush me, remind me I don't have to carry it all myself. You are always here to listen, to pick up my burdens and carry me home. Amen.

Taking Care

Learning to Mother

Kim

I give you a new commandment, that you love one another. Just as I have loved you, you also should love one another.

—John 13:34

stand at the edge of Charlotte's bedroom door, hand poised to switch the light off, only minutes away from being able to rest. The days are full and by this time at night, I can feel the comfort of our couch and the chance to sit in silence.

"It's time for bed. Lay down now, Charlotte."

"I'm not done yet, Mama." Oblivious to my hurry, Charlotte takes her time. She gently lifts her Elsa baby doll to her lips for a kiss before placing her on her sleeping bag and covering her head so it's just peeking out from the covers. Next to Elsa she lays her pink giraffe, two friends keeping each other company. Charlotte bends down to fluff the blankets and offers one more kiss.

I'm still anxious to flip off the switch, but her actions make me pause. I marvel at the care she's giving to her toys. They are not simply toys to her, but companions and friends in need of comfort.

My daughter's actions remind me what it means to care for those things we love. Her eyes don't leave Elsa and the giraffe—providing them comfort is what she desires in this moment. At night she gets the chance to practice tucking someone in and to offer the love she's been given in her nighttime routine. When you watch your children, maybe you see them doing things the way you do: making beds, building blocks, organizing books, dressing, and making food. Our children are always watching our actions, and in these moments we share our love.

There always seems to be a to-do list running through my head. The things that need to get done for the house, for food, for the kids, for my writing, and what I'd like to do for just me. In the midst of one activity, I'm thinking of what is to come next. In my daughter's room, at this moment, there's nowhere else to be. I suddenly forget what I planned to do when the kids were asleep and my desire for rest fades.

But it's precisely my children, the ones I'm with at the moment, who remind me to stay present. Focused. Motherhood turns our attention to the tiny people right in front of us. Our needs are so intertwined with theirs. Our hopes and dreams bound to their lives, and the life being built as a family. Our children do that to us over and over again—remind us how to care for one another.

While watching my children I am reminded that the small, daily acts of love I offer are being used to build a foundation. Your days, too, mama, are dripping with actions done in love. The way you prepare food, the clothes you set out the night before, the way you greet your neighbors on walks, and how you hang pictures on the wall—all point to attention and care. This is what mothers do: we tend and love.

Charlotte finally hops into bed, satisfied that Elsa and her giraffe are comfortable. Covering herself with blankets, I see her take one final look at her toys before she turns to me, "Tuck me in, Mama."

I walk to her bed, lean in and kiss her, just as she did to her toys, and give thanks for the small moments of wonder and learning.

My daughter has reminded me to take time for the ones we love.

PRACTICE

Together with your children, brainstorm small acts of love you can do for others. Perhaps you'll make cards for the local nursing home, deliver bread or cookies to a neighbor, volunteer at the animal shelter, or write encouraging messages with chalk on the sidewalks.

PRAYER

Dear God,
help me to love others
as you have loved me.
May all I do
be done in love:

dressing kids and folding laundry
preparing meals and packing lunch boxes
changing diapers and washing bodies
rocking babies back and forth.

You first loved us,
creating us and this world
and so we love others
over and over
from our rising
to our sleeping
clothed in your grace
forever and ever.
Amen.

How We Measure

Comparison

Erin

I pray that you may have the power to comprehend, with all the saints, what is the breadth and length and height and depth, and to know the love of Christ that surpasses knowledge, so that you may be filled with all the fullness of God.

–Ephesians 3:18-19

After I got pregnant, I lost myself in the mesmerizing world of Momfluencers. I scrolled through square after square of motherly excellence: heart-melting images of designer-clad babies, perfectly styled nurseries, and stunning family portraits. I wanted that shiny life, but I didn't realize how unattainable the sum of those images was until I actually became a mother.

When Jack was a toddler, I got a text from my husband and knew something was wrong. *Jack's underweight,* he wrote. *He's in the 16th percentile or something.*

Standing in my cubicle at work, I cringed. *What did the doctor say?* I texted back.

She kept drilling me about what he eats and drinks, he replied. *They want him to start drinking nutritional shakes.*

I sank into my office chair and stared out the window—I wasn't feeding our son the right food. I wasn't feeding him enough. *I* wasn't... enough.

This wasn't the first time I'd felt this way. Once my son's teacher reported that he'd been tripping too much at preschool and maybe he should get involved in some sort of physical activity. Another time our expensive sleep consultant suggested I'd nursed my son to sleep for too long and "ruined" his ability to fall asleep independently.

Have you ever felt like this? Maybe your child has a physical issue that keeps you checking "norms," or perhaps you're facing behavioral difficulties.

Perhaps you're wrestling with challenges at school or on the sports field. You might be facing a diagnosis that will change your child's life and wondering how you'll ever cope. It's easy to get caught up comparing ourselves to the families that surround us—in real life and online—and become discouraged.

Motherhood metrics seem to follow us at every stage: hours slept, diapers changed, amount of feedings. Raising kids can be so thankless, and sometimes it feels good to know we're measuring up to others. But what happens when we don't?

Sometimes we cry, we lose sleep, we delve into a late-night Google search. I've done it all. After receiving news about Jack's weight issues, I turned to the parents in my circle: One dad sent me the name of a registered dietitian who wrote on a balanced approach to toddler mealtime. Another mom shared about her daughter's picky eating. My grandma told me a story about my uncle, who's now the most adventurous eater among his siblings.

The more I listened to others' stories, the more I realized that the mom-fluencers I followed weren't telling the whole story of motherhood. Not the struggles over meals nor the tantrum taming. Not the soul-crushing middle of the night worries nor the constant stacks of paperwork. They'd hidden those messes from the frame. I wondered what else they'd hidden, and how the picture-perfect life they presented was doing more harm than good. What's more, in covering up the unsightly, had they hidden some of motherhood's beauty, too?

Whenever I'm tempted to measure motherhood, I remember that our faith tells us a different story: Motherhood is not a race to be won or a course to be aced or a song to be mastered. Motherhood is a sacred calling.

Our efforts to answer this call cannot be contained in tiny squares or report cards. Motherhood is more like a pilgrimage, a symphony, a sprawling mural we're continually painting. It's a thousand little acts of service—removing splinters, buttoning raincoats, wiping bottoms—most unseen, and many impossible to measure.

How do you capture a love as wide and wild as the sea?

Whatever doubts you're facing, whatever fears you have about your children, know that God designed you perfectly to mother your children. God walks with us through the hard places and loves us fiercely and without condition. God's love for us is endless.

TO PONDER

Be honest: How do you measure your worth as a mother? How does God see you?

PRAYER

Inhale: When I feel as if I'm not enough,
Exhale: God, let your grace pour into me.

A LESSON FROM HIDE-AND-SEEK
CONNECTING WITH GOD

Kim

Seek the LORD while he may be found, call upon him while he is near.

–Isaiah 55:6

With a smile on her face and the full force of her four-year-old voice Charlotte yells, "Hide-and-seek!" She runs to the dining room while covering her eyes and sitting down in one fell swoop. "One, two, three, four... hide-and-seek!" Isaac stands in place, his feet stomping up and down, while she counts. He can't seem to decide where to go. "Ready?! Hide-and-seek," she yells again prompting Isaac to turn and run down the hall away from his sister.

Hide-and-seek rarely fails to gain the attention of my kids. Charlotte runs down the hallway and bursts into rooms. Isaac is always trailing behind her, happy to be by her side. They make up their own rules, running back and forth and counting to ten every few minutes. At the park with friends someone suggests hide-and-seek, and all the kids take off in different directions. "One, two, three! Hide-and-seek!" I sometimes wonder if they just like to hear their voices yell this declaration.

Most Sundays after church, it's a free-for-all for my children. After the hour or so of wrangling, snack-providing, and juggling of kids, crayons, books, and toys, I'm ready for a few minutes to relax. They usually find their friends and chase one another around the sanctuary and between the pews. They even know where to find the extra communion bread. One Sunday as it was time to head home, Charlotte turned to me: "Hide-and-seek, Mama?"

A laugh came out of my mouth, "No, we're not playing hide-and-seek *here*. We're going home."

What is it in the game of hiding and seeking that brings such joy? What is it in loud voices counting, quiet breaths hiding, and the cheers of finding friends that delights at so many ages? When my kids find each other there's always an element of surprise, even if they can still see each other. I remember this surprise from my own youth group nights playing hide-and-seek. There was the pride in securing the best spot. There was the accomplishment of being the one to find your friends. There was the comradery joining together to find that last person.

Could it be that our whole life of faith feels like a game of hide-and-seek? We desire to know God and to have a relationship, we want to find that spark of hope, and find the overwhelming gift of grace that is ours for the taking. We want to be found and known by friends and family, really known in all our brokenness, insecurities, and fears. We want to be sought out by the One who first breathed life into this world and us. And we want to help others find this amazing grace and love that transcends time and place.

So perhaps the church is precisely the place where we should be playing hide-and-seek. Maybe the church teaches us repeatedly what it means to be found in Christ—fully known, fully loved, fully claimed as God's beloved child. Maybe we need the help of others to find this joy and this love in God, inviting our friends to play with us, and knowing we're not alone in the searching.

Another day at the park, Charlotte tires of the swings and runs to me, "Hide-and-seek, Mama?"

Yes, my love, go and hide. For you are always found in God.

PRACTICE

Play hide-and-seek with your children. Laugh and run together. Count out loud and every time you find one another give thanks to God who will never tire of finding you.

PRAYER

Ever-present God, you are never far from me. Yet, sometimes I forget this truth. I forget that you breathed life into me. I feel alone. When I'm uncertain and afraid, keep coming to me. When I'm unsure of myself, keep coming to me. Even when I feel lost, help me trust that I am found in you. You know me and love me, just as I am. Amen.

THE BEAUTY OF CHRISTMAS
FIRST CHURCH PAGEANT

Erin

For a child has been born for us,
a son given to us;
authority rests upon his shoulders;
and he is named
Wonderful Counselor, Mighty God,
Everlasting Father, Prince of Peace.

—Isaiah 9:6

With a whoosh of wind, we opened the door to our sanctuary. Poinsettias clustered the altar, wreaths decked the walls, and a shining Christmas tree towered beside the organ. Our two-year-old Jack's eyes grew wide as he took in the decorations. High-pitched giggles and chatter beckoned us forward into the fellowship hall. It was nearly time for the children's Christmas pageant to begin.

I helped Jack into his gray smock and Jack's Sunday school teacher handed him his mask. Jack was playing the part of the barn cat, one of the animals who witnessed Jesus' birth.

On Christmas Eve in our congregation, children become the preachers and act out the Christmas story in worship. It's a chance for them to imagine themselves in Jesus' time and walk through the turning point in God's love story with humanity. God's love comes to us embodied in baby Jesus, and life will never be the same.

Moms know this well: A baby changes everything.

Our pastor prayed over the group, then the Sunday school teachers ushered the parents out. We took our place in the pews, eager for worship to begin. This was Jack's first year participating, and my husband Jay and I sat on the edge of our seats watching to see if he'd fare alright. Given his age, I hoped he'd simply follow his part and not get stage fright.

Silver halos bobbed as the children sang out, "Go tell it on the mountain, that Jesus Christ was born!" A cluster of brown-smocked boys huddled in imaginary fields as amazed shepherds. Clutching his barn cat mask, Jack paraded through the sanctuary in a gaggle of barn animals.

But at one point in the performance, Jack began to take off his smock in the middle of a Christmas song. "No Jack-Jack, no," I murmured, clutching my husband's hand. I was equal parts humored and anxious.

But the show must go on, and go on it did, with Jack and the other children standing at the foot of Jesus' manger. They gazed with reverence at the little babe who was cast to play the part of Jesus, and through their eyes, we saw Jesus' birth story anew. And when the final Christmas hymn was sung, the congregation gave the children a round of applause for their efforts. Our little barn cat beamed with pride.

PRACTICE

God's inviting us to live the Christmas story and share it with others. Find a way to bring the story to life for your children: This Christmas, attend or perform in a Christmas pageant. Read Luke 2:1-21 aloud to them at bedtime, and if they're reading age, encourage them to read the lines of the angels. Or find a nativity set and have them act out the story while you read from a children's Bible.

PRAYER

Thank you, God, for the beauty of Christmas—
for the most holy night on which your son
was born, a sign of hope, grace embodied.
Thank you, God, for our children—
who lead us to marvel at the Christ child.
May we hold fast to our sense of wonder,
may we never tire of living the story,
sharing God's love with everyone we meet.
Amen.

GRIEF AND MEMORIES
HONORING LOVED ONES

Kim

And all the people responded with a great shout when they praised the LORD because the foundation of the house of the LORD was laid. But many of the priests and Levites and heads of families, old people who had seen the first house on its foundations, wept with a loud voice when they saw this house, though many shouted aloud for joy, so that the people could not distinguish the sound of the joyful shout from the sound of the people's weeping, for the people shouted so loudly that the sound was heard far away.

—Ezra 3:11-13

My dad died a few months before my wedding. Every year on his birthday and on the day he died, I desire to honor him and his life. I struggle to know how to tell my kids about my dad or how to keep his memory alive. Usually the grand plans I have for bringing out pictures, making a cake, and taking a long car ride in his honor never play out. More often than not, the days end up resembling all our other days: feeding and caring for kids, playing and reading books, loving and asking for forgiveness.

Sometimes my grief for my dad shows up in subtle moments: reading an inscription he wrote for me in a book, jazz music playing on the radio, or seeing my kids play with their toy trains. Some days bring a flood of memories in remembrance. I wish he could witness what I am now experiencing—the life I've built with my family. I look at my children and our life and see his presence and love all around. Joy and sorrow mingle in these moments, and I hold them together. My tears can and do witness to both and in certain moments it's hard to distinguish which is which.

Maybe for you, it's a parent or a sibling, or a beloved friend from your childhood. Maybe there's the uncle or aunt you'd love for your children to know. Whoever it is that is no longer on this earth, we want to share them with our children, and for our kids to know the gift of their love. There's the grief that comes from seeing our life now and wishing they were here to witness it with us: our children's milestones, summer ice cream at the park, and holidays around the table. In our children's eyes or the way they laugh, we see our loved ones. I'm learning the way to remember my dad isn't about the grand adventures or specific days laced with meaning, but rather living my day-to-day life and feeling his presence with us.

In life and death, God's love binds us together for all time and in all places. In my tradition we give thanks for the communion of saints, those who have gone before us and those who are to come. The love of our creator touches everyone and everything. Take a moment today and remember your loved one. Tell them what's on your heart. Trust that their love is with you this day and forever more.

PRACTICE

If you have family and friends who have died and you'd like to share about them with your children, find some pictures or mementos from your time with your loved ones. Talk about them with your children. Don't wait for a special day or occasion, but tell your kids how their legacy of love lives on.

PRAYER

God of all time and all places, your love reaches beyond our understanding. Our loved ones are with us even when their bodies are no longer on this earth. It's a mystery and a gift. We give thanks for those who have died. As we grieve and remember, help us to trust that their love reaches us, and that they are never far from us. In Jesus' name we pray. Amen.

SHE TAUGHT ME
TO MOTHER
MOTHERING MENTORS

Erin

Strength and dignity are her clothing,
and she laughs at the time to come.

–Proverbs 31:25

A
t least once daily, I sing to my children. I'll belt out "Let it go" during a *Frozen* dance party, croon "Rubber Ducky, you're the one!" at bath time or hum "Jesus loves me, this I know" into their ears at bedtime.

Years ago, as a new mom, I assumed this habit came from years of choir and voice lessons. I treasured the chance to share my love for music with my newborn.

Then my mother came to visit again. I gladly handed her Jack and retreated to the bedroom for a much-needed nap. A couple hours later I woke, roused by the sound of my mother's voice. It was soft, nearly a whisper. She was singing "Jesus Loves Me" to my son and rocking him to sleep in his nursery. That's when it dawned on me: I sing to Jack because she sang to me.

She taught me to mother through countless games of catch and stories read. She sat in the audience at choir concerts, musicals, and softball games. For my birthday, she still serves my favorite treat—pumpkin pie with extra whip cream. She ends our conversations with the words "I love you." And now, she shows up on my doorstep to care for me and my children.

My mother's love is a favorite song; its melody plays back to me in the ways I mother. And she's not the only one who's influenced my mothering:

My grandmothers, both pillars of faith, taught me to pray at the dinner table. They fed my belly with spaghetti, chicken noodle soup, press cookies and zucchini bread, and fed my soul by sharing devotionals. Their love is a prayer, wrapping me in love and holding me close when I need a reminder of faithfulness.

My dear friend Megan taught me the value of hospitality. She opened her home to me dozens of times and gathered friends around the table for baked nachos, Thai stir-fry, fellowship, and card games. Her love is an invitation, an open door, a bigger table.

My therapist helped me learn to accept all my emotions. She is an endless well of grace from which I draw to better understand myself and others. Her love is a listening ear, a guiding question, full acceptance.

My pastor, Kelly, knows how to mark special moments and make people, especially children, feel seen and appreciated. Her love is a burst of confetti, a bunch of balloons, a celebration.

Then there's Ruth and Naomi from the Bible, who taught me the value of loyalty. Ruth, who told her mother-in-law Naomi, "Where you go, I will go; where you lodge, I will lodge; your people shall be my people, and your God my God. Where you die, I will die—there will I be buried" (Ruth 1:16-17). Their love is a pact, feet on the ground, togetherness.

When I think about all the influences that affect my mothering, my heart swells with joy. I can clearly see their presence in my life—through song, prayers, open doors, confetti, and loyalty—reflected in the way I nurture my children. Love offered and shared again and again, pointing me back to an ever-loving God.

TO PONDER

Who taught you how to mother? What lessons do you bring to your children because of the love you received from other mothers and mother-figures? Take a moment to reflect and give thanks to God for their presence.

PRAYER

Source of all love,
you've gifted me a wellspring
of mothers and mother figures
each one a thread woven
into the tapestry of my life—

a life of love, grief, and beauty.
Be with me now as I weave
love into the lives of my children
and may all my labors thread
their hearts back to you.
Amen.

GOD'S MASTERPIECE
MOTHERHOOD AND CREATIVITY

Kim

For we are what he has made us, created in Christ Jesus for good
works, which God prepared beforehand to be our way of life.

–Ephesians 2:10

Many afternoons the light pours through our living room window
cascading rainbows on our carpet, walls, and dining room table.
During the after-school-before-dinner hours (when everyone is
tired, hungry, and could use a nap) we either take a walk or do some creating.
My kids love to create—painting, coloring, cutting paper, tracing, or sculpting
Play-Doh.

One afternoon, at the table with paper and pencils scattered and brushes
of paint ready, I overhear Isaac telling his sister, "Come on Charlotte, let's make
our masterpieces."

Isaac grips a marker with his left hand making a truck with a crane on top
to do its important work. Charlotte starts with a rainbow and ice cream cones.
They fill up sheet after sheet and soon hunt for the tape so they can hang their
masterpieces in our hallway. Kids have an innate sense that what they create is
good and worthy to be seen. Before even the first stroke of the marker, my kids
know that they can and will create a masterpiece. Creating in and of itself is the
gift, the masterpiece. And so are we.

When we're in seasons where we don't know what day it is and are unable
to remember the last time we took a shower or sat down for a meal, we are the
ones who need the reminder that we are God's masterpiece. Nothing more and
nothing less than God's beloved child. As mothers it can feel like the work we
do is tedious, and it may be hard to find meaning in preparing food, changing
diapers, and building blocks with our children. Yet, all we do from conjuring stories at bedtime to helping with homework and shuttling to and from

practices is an act of creation. We're creating community and inspiring the hearts and minds of our children.

I'm learning from my children to first and foremost remember the masterpiece I am, and from that knowledge to simply create; to do what brings me joy and to look upon it with eyes of appreciation.

We are all God's masterpieces. We have been created in love to love and to be loved. There's nothing we must do or be—only rest in the name God places on us, beloved child of God. Clothed with this knowledge, basking in this love, go out and see the world in all its infinite beauty and goodness. Go out and dream, create, and splash beauty and hope across all you meet.

PRACTICE

Create something! Grab markers, paper, Play-Doh, yarn, or fabric and make something for the joy of creating.

PRAYER

Creator God, you fashion me from your image and call me good. I am the work of your hands. I am loved. I am beautiful. Help me to see myself as you see me, and to then go out and bring forth beautiful creations. Amen.

ENJOYING THE CRUMBS
OUR "GOOD OLD DAYS"

Erin

Then Jesus laid his hands on [the blind man's] eyes again; and he
looked intently and his sight was restored, and he saw everything
clearly.

—Mark 8:25

"These are the good old days…"

From my spot in the coffee shop, I looked up from my smartphone. The speaker was an older gentleman with twinkling eyes, nodding in the direction of my bumbling two-year-old.

"I'm sorry?" I said, not following him. I'd been checking the time, calculating how much longer I could let Jack explore the coffee shop.

"These are the good old days," he repeated wistfully. He smiled and watched my son wander around our local coffee shop.

"Oh yes!" I chuckled, taking a swig of my latte and glancing at our table. A pile of banana bread crumbs and an empty juice box lay there, abandoned.

I wanted to tell the man that I knew this, that this is exactly why we came here on a Wednesday before I went to work and dropped my son off at daycare. I wanted to tell him that I didn't get enough moments like this, that I was determined to savor the heck out of this moment, but my son was now blocking the doorway and well, I could see he'd left a trail of crumbs that started at our table and ended where he was now standing expectantly.

Jack stared me down. "Mommy, let's GO!" The force in his voice caused a few more coffee drinkers to lift their eyes. I could tell he was on the verge of a meltdown.

"Yes, let's go, buddy," I said. In one swift motion, I dropped my latte in the trash and reached for Jack's hand. But the crumbs… Did I mention the crumbs? The crumbs were everywhere.

"Honey, one sec, we need to clean up," I said, swiping the counter clean with my free hand.

By the time I'd finished, the gentleman had left. But I couldn't stop thinking about what he had said, wondering what he meant by, "these are the good old days."

Tucking my son into his car seat, I considered it. Driving to his daycare and singing along to Elmo's alphabet rap, I turned it over in my head. Kneeling before my son and putting on his tiny sneakers, I thought of it. Only when I brushed the crumbs from my child's lips and kissed him on the cheek before I whispered, "I love you, have a good day," did it dawn on me: the old man was right: the good old days are now, but I was so caught up in my rush to get to work I nearly missed it.

Your good old days are now, too, showing up in what we often might consider life's crumbs. Tiny details of our ordinary days that seem so commonplace we barely notice when they fade into the background: your child's favorite song, your rituals for saying goodbye, the special one-to-one time you plan for them. The ways your children show their love, even the challenging moments like tantrums, are all ephemeral as they age and change.

When Jesus placed his hands on the blind man's eyes, his sight was restored. That's what I think God's doing for us in our ordinary moments. God's asking us to see clearly what's before us, extraordinary treasures brimming with grace.

I don't think God's asking us to savor every moment (after all, I didn't mind so much when, years later, we were done with diapers), but I do think there's wisdom in those words, in attending to the "crumbs" that define our kids in this season and seeing their sacredness. Those sacred crumbs point us back to a God who's always nearby, looking on us with love, gifting us with our "good old days."

PRACTICE

Pick up a pen and take a moment to write down what life looks like right now: are you scraping up crumbs and taming tantrums? Acting as the tooth fairy? Snuggling children who wake in the middle of the night and need comfort from you? Capture this moment in time, your own "good old days." Thank God for the beauty of motherhood, for miracles hidden in the mundane.

PRAYER

God,
these are our good old days—
days of crumbs on the carpet
of tucking the covers just so
and planting kisses on our children's foreheads
of well-worn shirts and toys scattered across the carpet
soccer cleats and socks crowding the doorways
ballet shoes abandoned in the basement
crayoned art hung on the fridge
and picture books stacked on the nightstand
of *Sesame Street* and *Paw Patrol*
and favored stuffies
days of hope, grace, love, forgiveness
of feeling your love in the arms of our children
God, these are the good old days
give me eyes to see your presence
woven into the fabric of our ordinary existence.
Amen.

Your Heart is a Garden
Seasons of Growth

Kim

Then God said, "Let the earth put forth vegetation: plants yielding seed and fruit trees of every kind on earth that bear fruit with the seed in it." And it was so. The earth brought forth vegetation: plants yielding seed of every kind and trees of every kind bearing fruit with the seed in it. And God saw that it was good. And there was evening and there was morning, the third day.

–Genesis 1:11-13

January Garden Report // At first look there doesn't seem to be much growth. The air is cold and the sun's light is scant these days. Plenty of nights have dipped below freezing. The last weed was picked in early fall, and nothing else has grown. Today we dumped compost and manure on the garden. A drop of a shovel here, and a prayer for the months to come. The winter days provide rest for the ground, nutrients seeping into the earth, and the trust that all that is unseen will bear fruit in the seasons to come.

January Heart Report // At first look there doesn't seem to be any growth. The cold temperatures and lack of sun don't provide much motivation. There's weariness from sickness, uncertainty, and a constant vigilance against a world in unrest. Yet, a candle's light, the comfort of a blanket, and moments of simply being offer rest on these longer nights. There are journals filled with prayers and moments of God's presence. The early mornings are met with hot coffee, cheers from the kids, and God's word to comfort and inspire. Hope, peace, and joy seep into my body, and I, too, trust that all that is unseen will bear fruit in the seasons to come.

Spring Garden Report // The rain and cold temperatures keep our family from the garden. I know there's no rush to plant. The time will come when the ground is ripe for sowing seeds. In past years I've felt the pressure to get the plants and seeds in the ground, and too often in those years I found myself replanting. So this year, I wait. As a family we prepare the soil by pulling weeds and shaping the beds. We make a list of what we want to grow and how we want to share the bounty with others. And finally, when the sun dries the ground and the last frost is behind us, we plant seeds. Together with the kids, I make the rows and they drop sunflower and bean seeds one by one into the earth. We cover them with dirt, and we say a prayer.

Spring Heart Report // The world feels fragile. There's the weight I feel right now in my home: raising kind and caring kids, teaching respect, looking out for neighbors in need, sharing God's love. There's also the weight of the world: war and violence, political fighting, neighbors unable to look one another in the eye. The tasks before us seem insurmountable, but then I remember the ground and the seeds we planted one by one.

Every day we go and check the garden, finding we can count more weeds than actual plants. But one day, we see beans shooting up from the earth. Before us life reaches towards the sun. The kids cheer, "Beans, beans, beans!" What was unseen, seemingly lost in the ground has been brought into the light.

Perhaps this is the constant work of motherhood—sowing seeds of kindness, compassion, love, and grace into our children and our communities, and watching what bursts forth into the world.

PRACTICE

No matter the season, plant a seed with your family. Prepare the soil and container, plant the seed with a prayer, water, and wait. Give thanks for the work of creation that happens beyond what we can see. Give thanks for the darkness, and trust that God will bring new life.

PRAYER

God of creation, you're always making something new. You bring life out of death. You bring light into a world in need of your goodness. Help me to sow your peace, love, and gentleness. Open my eyes to the bounty of your love everywhere I go. Amen.

CHILDHOOD

A Gentler Approach to Mornings
Motherhood and Anger

Erin

...lead a life worthy of the calling to which you have been called, with all humility and gentleness, with patience, bearing with one another in love.

–Ephesians 4:1-2

"don't want to be the mom who yells," I sighed into the phone during a recent therapy session. "But Jack wouldn't listen. I lost it," I said, clenching and unclenching my fist. I told my therapist I apologized, but that I still feel horrible. That's when she suggested a talisman.

"Sounds like you need something to remind you how you want to be," she said, pausing to think. "Maybe something soft, like a scarf or a ribbon? A smooth stone you could keep in your pocket?"

"Or a piece of jewelry?" I offered. "Jack would love that!"

Gemstones and treasures fascinate my son. I knew just where I'd order: a company I admire that pairs Scripture with jewelry.

Ten days later, I unboxed a necklace and cradled it in my hands. Afternoon sun shone through the windows and glinted off its delicate chain.

"Mommy, what's that?" Jack asked, reaching towards me.

"My new necklace," I said, handing it to him. "Do you like it?"

"Yes!" he exclaimed, running his fingers over its soft pendant.

"Shall I try it on?" I said, taking the necklace back and draping it over my head. I raced to the mirror to admire it. A rose gold chain punctuated with a smooth beige tassel rested right above my heart—something soft "to remind me how I want to be."

Paired with my necklace came a Scripture card encouraging me to "...lead a life worthy of the calling to which you have been called, with all humility and gentleness, with patience, bearing with one another in love." (Ephesians 4:1-2). Would this necklace help me parent more gently, even in the toughest moments, reflecting God's compassion and love? I hoped so.

The next morning, when it was time for Jack to get dressed for preschool, my darling boy scrunched up his face as if he'd eaten a rotten egg. He yelled, "I DON'T WANNA go to school!" and threw himself on his bed, legs flailing.

I brushed my fingertips against my talisman's tassel and recalled my resolution. "Bear with him in love, bear with him in love," I murmured to myself. But how to get Jack out the door? I took a deep breath and fought the urge to bark a warning.

"You don't want to go to school, and it's making you feel upset," I said to my son. "I don't always want to go to work, either."

His voice quieted, though he continued whimpering. Jack really didn't want to go to school. Watching him struggle, I wondered about the opposite of shouting. For some strange reason, I thought, what would Mary Poppins do? Could I solve this with a song?

"Super Jack is going to school!" I sang, startling Jack out of his whining. (Superman is his favorite hero.) To my surprise, he crawled off his bed to receive my help getting dressed. For each step of our routine, I added new verses—Super Jack is putting on socks, brushing his teeth, etc. At each verse, his face brightened with glee.

An ordinary object made way for a holy, loving moment.

My talisman isn't a magic prescription for good behavior; in fact, it's more compass than cure. Despite my efforts, I'll always need grace and forgiveness. I keep looking to Scripture to remind me how I want to be. God, after all, is the gentlest parent. And God's grace stretches wide enough to fill in our gaps.

PRACTICE

How would you characterize your parenting style? Are there any patterns in your interactions with your children you'd like to amend? What do you like about the way you parent? Choose your own word or verse to focus on, then find or create your own talisman. Try carrying it with you during the week and touch it anytime you need encouragement. God loves to see you grow in your labors as a mother.

PRAYER

God of all gentleness,
when my children ignore me, it makes me angry.
Maybe that's how you feel when I ignore you, too.
Sometimes, I need a little reminder to soften my voice
or my posture. Sometimes, I need a little nudge to bear
with others in love. Help me orient my heart to you.
Bolster my patience with my kids—and myself.
Drench us in your grace. Amen.

"What'd You Have for Breakfast?"
Seasons of Connection

Kim

Jesus said to them, "Come and have breakfast." Now none of the disciples dared to ask him, "Who are you?" because they knew it was the LORD.

–John 21:12

Surrounded by plates of spaghetti and meatballs, glasses of water, and scraps of paper from a day of coloring, I bring the phone to the table and call the kids' grandparents. Across the distance, our family joins us for meals. Sometimes they have their own food, and other times we've caught them on the couch. The kids like to hide and pop out to say hello. But it never fails that after the initial "hellos" and "how are yous," Charlotte asks: "What'd you have for breakfast?"

We hear about Cheerios and bananas, bread with Nutella, and the occasional restaurant meal. The kids make their grandparents guess what they had for breakfast. Before we get to any other conversation, Charlotte asks about lunch and dinner. Every phone call repeats the same questions. "What'd you eat?" Our family delights in these conversations about the mundane and have come to expect them. We were made to be in community, and thanks to my daughter, I'm learning that distance doesn't have to be a barrier.

It's never just about breakfast. The calls or texts are about connection—seeing the lives of family even from a distance. Underlying Charlotte's questions is the subtext: *I love you. I want to know what you do and what you love.*

In any of our relationships we can practice the art of connecting no matter the distance. One of the lessons Jesus teaches us is that even though we move and travel, we can cultivate relationships with others. Christ set out a breakfast for the disciples on the beach as a way of reconnecting after an absence. We, too, can reach out to those in front of us, and those who are at a distance. We can write letters like Paul to encourage and pray for our family and friends. We can phone our family and ask them about breakfast, weaving connections and love through daily acts of writing and calling.

At the heart of Charlotte's question, lies the heart of cultivating relationships. Asking about breakfast is asking about the simple and ordinary moments of life, seeing how a life of faith is shaped in community, one small action at a time, one question at a time.

PRACTICE

Make a list of your community: family, friends, neighbors. Who haven't you connected with in a while? Set aside time for a phone or video call. While talking learn about the foods they love and how they spend their meals. Give thanks for the nourishment of food and family.

PRAYER

God of all places and time,
thank you for family and friends
for gathering over a meal
for technology that allows us to see and hear others
for the gift of Jesus' presence
with us at home
around the table
and across a screen.
Amen.

WATER AND LIGHT

MILESTONE: BAPTISM

Erin

...when you had heard the word of truth, the gospel of your salvation, and had believed in him, were marked with the seal of the promised Holy Spirit.

–Ephesians 1:13

"What's this, Mommy?"

My son held out a skinny red box he'd found in his closet, waiting for my reply.

"Hmm…" I said, taking the box and popping open the lid. Inside was a tall white candlestick with a dove on it. I handed it back to Jack. "It's a candle we lit the day you were baptized. Here, let me show you some pictures."

Jack's baptism took place at our church of many years, the community of faith we joined as a doe-eyed engaged couple.

My husband, who rarely dresses up, wore a tie, I wore a cream dress with flowers, and four-month-old Jack wore an outfit complete with baby suspenders. The sanctuary was sunny, warm, and filled with a buzzing congregation. Jack looked serene as our pastor baptized him with holy water.

"That's me?!" my son exclaimed, looking up from the photos. "What's baptized?"

I tell him that's a great question. "It's a way our church welcomes a baby into God's family. The water signifies the new life we have in Jesus."

What stuck with me most from Jack's baptism was that, after Jack's godparents, Jay, and I promised to share God's story with Jack, my fellow parishioners rose and promised to assist us. I'd recited this liturgy many times from the pews, but this was my first time receiving the words, and they washed over me like soft rain.

At times childrearing can feel incredibly lonely, but my church reminded Jay and me that we weren't alone in raising our son. Faith formation isn't a solo effort, rather, it's a group project, led by the Holy Spirit. As Jack grew, he would sing hymns and pray alongside our congregation. He'd receive Sunday school instruction from volunteers I knew and adored. His name would be lifted up in prayer by fellow congregants.

The words of the final blessing came back to me: "Jack Jason, you are marked by the Cross of Christ and sealed with the Holy Spirit." The Spirit was alive and working in our hearts. This beautiful truth hit me again as I sat alongside my son, who was twirling his baptism candle and looking up at me expectantly.

"Mommy, do you have a baptism candle?"

"I'm sure I do… but I need to find it," I said, rising to retrieve my phone. "I'll ask Grandma about that."

Water and light. These common, powerful elements serve as important symbols in our Christian tradition. Any time we dip our toes in a lake, step into a shower, or get caught in the rain can be cause to remember our baptism. The setting sun, the sparkling stars, and flickering firelight remind us of the Light of the world, who guides us.

As it turns out, my mom had saved my baptism candle, and now I store it with my son's. In the years to come, these candles will remind us of our place in God's family and the faith communities that bolster us. We'll light the wicks and give thanks for the waters of baptism. We'll watch them shine and trust that God's love will always shine for us.

TO PONDER

The sacrament of holy baptism is a tangible expression of God's unseen, ever-present grace, both for you and your children. How does your church family help your child remember their baptism? Who helps you remember your baptism? Give thanks for the body of Christ today.

PRAYER

Heavenly God, through baptism, you invite me into the church and wash me clean with your perfect love. Marked by your love, embolden me to walk into the world and spread your love to others. Amen.

Morning Quiet Time
Investing in the Mother

Kim

For God alone my soul waits in silence; from him comes my salvation. He alone is my rock and my salvation, my fortress; I shall never be shaken.

—Psalm 62:1-2

Sitting on the front porch, I focus on the purple petunias before me, their color illuminated against the blue sky. I watch the leaves dance to the wind's movement and with each bird song emanating from the trees, I feel my spirit linger in rest. Two hummingbirds dance before me at the feeder sipping their morning nectar. To my right, a small table holds a book of morning prayer, my Bible, a journal and pen, and my current devotional book. A few walkers pass, and their conversation floats in the air while cars make their way down the street. Inside my house, the kids eat their breakfast (on lucky days, they are still sleeping—but not today). I sip hot, freshly brewed coffee. I take a deep breath.

I've long had the desire to be an early morning riser to read and write. Since having children, the mornings come quickly and so do the requests for breakfast. I have sometimes been able to get up before the kids, but never regularly. Friends have shared over and over about the life changing magic of morning time, and I always had a hunch that I would come to love the practice. If only I could commit.

The summer my kids were six and three, I decided to not let any excuses get in my way. I made getting up early a priority so I could focus on myself and filling my own well. I took stock of small things that could add up to a smoother morning: setting the coffee to brew the night before (thanks to my husband!) and leaving my pile of books by the front door. By the time my alarm went off the first morning, I eagerly poured the coffee and sat on the front porch.

Whether the kids are awake or still sleeping, the goal is to show up on the porch regardless. If they're awake, I'll pour cereal and set them up for breakfast. Some mornings I'm able to eke out more than 15 minutes before the kids' opening and closing of the front door becomes too distracting. Every morning, though, I keep going to the porch to read and write. I highlight and underline words that jump out at me. Questions and prayers that arise find their way in my journal.

Throughout the summer, the hummingbirds come closer to me each morning. I wonder if they are getting braver, or if I am getting more still?

These moments of quiet contemplation, these moments of sitting and being, these moments of consuming before creating, can they be bold? Is it a bold thing to claim the morning hours for oneself before all others? Is it bold to greet the morning with hope and intention, settling into the day, receiving it as a gift. Is it bold to declare that I am worthy of rest and solitude and quiet mornings dripping with grace?

I hope so. I believe so. As mothers we need to take care of ourselves. The daily tasks and to-do's can consume us if we let them. Getting swept into the needs of our children and the demands of our callings as partners and mothers can consume our time. But there is a way, with intention and small steps, to make space for ourselves.

In my practice of waking early, I'm feeling a renewed energy to greet the day. I'm modeling a bold faith found in quiet moments pondering God's Word, finding refreshment in the silence, and trusting the unseen work that's refining my soul. I also believe that setting apart this time and inviting my children to see these small, meaningful acts, allows them to know the power of rest. The mornings serve as a reminder of how loved by God I am, so that I am poised to share that love with my children.

You too, mama, can be bold to take time for you. To rest in God's grace that says no matter what you do or don't do, no matter how many the to-do's, no matter how frazzled you feel, you are loved. You are worth caring for yourself.

PRACTICE

What's one small act you can do for yourself every day or every night? Brainstorm ways to care for your mind and body and choose one (five minutes of quiet outside, a quick walk, reading, cup of tea, calling a friend, etc.) Commit to this one small act and ponder how God meets you in this ritual.

PRAYER

Dear God, the world is full of things to do and people who desire my attention. The needs of my children and partner are always before me. I want to be there for them and for others, but I need moments for me, too. Help me to rest my body and mind. Help me to be bold in declaring time for me. Teach me to see myself as worthy of care and love. Give me rest. Give me peace. In Jesus' name, I pray. Amen.

THE MIRACLE OF REST
SELF-CARE FOR MOMS

Erin

Come to me, all you that are weary and are carrying heavy burdens, and I will give you rest.

–Matthew 11:28

Before the COVID-19 pandemic, I was constantly in motion—rising early to beat the call of "Mommy!"; gulping down hot coffee; rushing to and from preschool and the office; racing through bedtime stories only to crash into bed, exhausted. As a working mom, I wanted to do it all and do it well. I failed, yet I kept moving.

Underneath my hustling, I longed to be the kind of mom who was present and unhurried, but I often felt as if there were too many demands of my time to slow down and rest in the love of God and my family.

Then COVID-19 upended my habits. Suddenly I was working from home and caring for my son, and while the tension of this produced additional stress, it was also a hidden gift. When we were forced to stay home during the pandemic, Jack and I could linger in bed on a Tuesday morning and discuss our dreams. Stay in our pajamas. Savor juicy blueberry pancakes and the view outside our window before I picked up my laptop and he played with Magna-Tiles. Outside our window was a tree I began to notice—red pinpricks flecked its branches in early spring before becoming pale green buds that unfurled into cream-colored blossoms.

My son Jack blossomed, too. He'd begun counting and recognizing letters. Snuggled under his comforter, he told epic bedtime tales of imaginary treasure hunts, races, and rescue missions. Jack traded his red balance bike for an orange "big boy bike" with training wheels. Together we'd twirl around the living room, accompanied by "Into the Unknown" and other songs from the *Frozen 2* soundtrack. On Sundays, we'd sit side by side on the couch and worship with our congregation via Zoom. Jack could move freely, play, and ask questions while taking in the service, none of which I felt comfortable with when we attended church in person.

I witnessed it all. Miracle.

That year reshaped the way I understood rest. More and more I'm learning that rest is a spiritual discipline, one that we can only take on when we surrender our work.

Rest is the pause that we take when we stop pouring out for others and fill up our own cups. Rest is waiting for you, a gift from God you don't have to earn: You are worthy of rest right now.

Many women have been conditioned to think rest doesn't apply to us. We hear "a mother's work is never finished," and we see it in our cluttered counters, endless to-do lists, and late nights caring for sick children. God invites us to lay down our work and bask in God's love. The move toward rest is one I resist, yet when I engage in it, rest revives my soul with goodness.

Jesus rested. He stepped away from his ministry from time to time and prayed. Moreover, he calls us to do the same. I find this truth helpful to remember in the fleeting hour before my bedtime, a window of time I can use to recharge or to accomplish more work. Often my first thought is to use that time to finish a task before I allow myself to relax—ordering new shoes for my sons, polishing a piece of writing, picking up Legos from the playroom carpet. When I choose to rest, I like to journal about my day, read a novel or watch a favorite streaming series. Occasionally I put myself to bed early or practice yoga.

Rest says the task list can wait and your body needs renewal. Rest says, let God be God and you be you. Rest says it is holy to slow down and find peace. In a bustling world, rest is God beckoning us to abide with God in stillness.

PRACTICE

Try implementing a weekly family sabbath discipline. On Sundays—or another sabbath day that works for your schedule—set aside chores and revel in spending time with each other. Go to worship, eat takeout, disconnect from technology, and move your bodies. Take a quiet hour for yourself doing something that feels good for you.

PRAYER

Inhale: God, your love is constant.

Exhale: I don't need to earn rest.

Inhale: May I set aside my tasks.

Exhale: And abide in your presence.

WORSHIPING
WITH CHILDREN
FAITH FORMATION

Kim

And let us consider how to provoke one another to love and good deeds, not neglecting to meet together, as is the habit of some, but encouraging one another, and all the more as you see the Day approaching.

—Hebrews 10:24-25

With donut-filled cheeks and sticky fingers, Charlotte and Isaac skip down the hallway in front of me to find a seat in church. With a smile the usher greets us at the door. "Morning!" He offers the bulletin to me while two small hands reach up with a chorus of "me too's" and "mine." The organ's deep notes pipe through the sanctuary and welcome me to the space. Piling into the pew each child voices their own demand. "Mommy sit next to me," Charlotte pleads as Isaac quickly yells, "No me!" I drop the diaper bag, bulletins, and my purse. We all sit as the music continues to play.

While I worked as a pastor, children in worship never bothered or distracted me. Kids who cried or melted down, ran up to the front of the church, or talked loudly were always a joy to see and hear. I reveled at the gift of their presence.

Yet, as a mom with my own children, my patience is easily tested. Every sound they make feels like shouting through a megaphone. What could be considered cute and funny at home (counting together, saying their ABC's, or climbing all over me) drives me crazy at church. I know from conversations with other parents that everyone struggles to focus in worship with young kids. I can't help but see other families (or at least the picture of them I have in my mind) with kids coloring quietly or listening without an arsenal of snacks at the ready. Many Sundays, sitting in the pews with my kids, I feel like I'm not measuring up.

Even though my insecurity sometimes tells me differently, I don't actually know a family who sits perfectly in church every single Sunday. I don't know one parent who hasn't wrestled their kids in the pews or faced a toddler wanting to take their clothes and shoes off in worship, or listened to the never-ending question of wanting another donut. Worship with children is loud, exhausting, and a sometimes-never-ending-wrestling match.

If I really take the time to see the people next to me, I see families just like me doing the hard and holy work of raising their kids in faith.

If I were to pastor my present self, I would say to give myself more grace. I'd repeat: *You're doing great. We're glad you're here. We know it takes so much, but it's worth it, and most importantly, God is with you.*

God doesn't measure how loud or unruly our children are; rather, God's marveling at the sheer beauty and energy of their lives. God doesn't measure the number of Cheerios needed to keep children quiet; rather, God's marveling at the families who are able to show up week after week. God doesn't measure how much we get out of the hymns, Bible readings, and sermons; rather, God's marveling at all of us as beloved, precious gifts—the work of our creator's hands. And when we're not able to attend worship, God continues to meet us wherever we are.

The next time I worship with my family may be just as challenging and tiring for me, but we'll be there, together. We'll be there in the pew with Cheerios and pencils and fidgety bodies. That's one of the messages I hope my children receive from worship week after week—we're there showing up as a family. And marveling in the measure of God's love and grace that encompasses us all.

PRACTICE

Next time you attend worship as a family, reflect on the people who are there to support you. Give thanks for the hands that offer to hold your baby, the treats that are given to your kids, the Sunday school teachers who share faith, and the other families who continue to show up week after week. Remember that you are not alone in raising your children to know and love God.

PRAYER

God of stillness and movement,
song and dance,
liturgy and silence,
Cheerios and coffee.
You meet me in worship
whether at home or in the pews,
in my understanding and doubt.
Your presence is known.
Thank you for communities
who welcome
and love
and open their arms to children.
Draw us closer to you
with every song and prayer
in Jesus' name, we pray.
Amen.

"Mommy, Follow Me!"

Catching Faith
from our Children

Erin

> But ask the animals, and they will teach you;
> the birds of the air, and they will tell you;
>
> ask the plants of the earth, and they will teach you;
> and the fish of the sea will declare to you.
>
> Who among all these does not know
> that the hand of the LORD has done this?
>
> In [God's] hand is the life of every living thing
> and the breath of every human being.
>
> —Job 12:7-10

Nature church started accidentally. Some mishap at home I can no longer remember—was it a power struggle over socks? spilled cereal?—left us scrambling out the door to church. Once we finally began our commute, I realized that if my son and I continued course, we would be embarrassingly late to worship.

"Well," I remember telling Jack as I switched on our car blinker, "It looks like we're going to nature church today." With that, I changed lanes and put us on the path to our local nature preserve, a place we both loved to visit.

Walking into the wooded sanctuary, I told Jack, "God created everything here, even you and me, and called it good. Isn't that wonderful?" He nodded vigorously; he had heard the creation story before. That served as our sermon, then we took turns marveling at trees, toads, and birds. We sat to enjoy a sacred snack of applesauce pouches. Then we picked dandelion puffs and blew prayers into the wind.

The next Sunday, Jack wanted to go back to nature church, but I wanted to attend "regular church." As a compromise, we agreed to keep sabbath outdoors once monthly.

One wet Sunday in December, the wind was especially bitter and the path was puddle studded. I sat in the car for a while and considered changing plans. "Are we doing nature church?" Jack called out from his car seat. I took a deep breath and steeled myself. "I guess so," I relented.

Donning heavy jackets and snow boots, we tip-toed around icy puddles until we reached a bridge to higher ground that looked significantly less mushy.

Jack raced into the barren forest. "Mommy, follow me!" he cried, ambling up the hill ahead of us. I could not see what was over the bend. Where was he taking us?

"Wait for me, buddy!" I gasped, charging up the hill with my arms and legs swinging. Jack ran back from the crest and smiled down at me, his cheeks rosy.

"Follow me!" he repeated.

Soon, we were at the foot of a fallen tree trunk, Jack crouching to examine a patch of moss. I couldn't help but think he'd adopted a posture of prayer. I crouched down alongside him.

"What's this, Mommy?" Jack said, running his gloves against the moss. Green popped against black-brown bark, a burst of color amid a muted landscape.

"It's beautiful," I breathed, touching the patch of green. Jack looked at me quizzically. "I mean, it's moss," I added.

We continued our adventures. I followed Jack's lead in seeking every sign of life in those wintry woods. We straddled tree trunks, listened to the river chorus, and felt blood course through our bodies as we braved the cold and explored the wilderness. When afternoon shifted to evening, we watched the sun drop to the west. Gold light weaved in and out of dark branches, dappling crisp leaves and warming our faces.

I used to think the point of nature church was for me to teach my son about creation. I wanted him to know that everything from the soaring geese to the tiniest patch of moss bears our Creator's signature. Yet, Jack's wonder at each turn continues to inspire *me*.

"Mommy, follow me!" he always says. And, I do.

PRACTICE

Visit a local preserve or park and create your own nature church—for yourself or with your children. Bring a Bible along and some snacks. Allow yourselves to wander where the Spirit leads you. Read your Bible or pray aloud. Take turns hunting for beauty in the created world. Give thanks to God for the gifts of creation.

PRAYER

God, the whole of creation is alive
singing your praises—
the babbling brook,
the wild geese,
the croaking toads,
the fields of wildflowers.
I, too, will praise your handiwork
and answer your call to steward it well.
Amen.

A Mother's Hands
Seasons of Change

Kim

Do you not know that your body is a temple of the Holy Spirit within you, which you have from God, and that you are not your own? For you were bought with a price; therefore glorify God in your body.

–1 Corinthians 6:19-20

Young mothers hear no shortage of comments and well-meaning advice about savoring the time with small children. "Babies don't keep!" "Enjoy them—they grow so fast." Even with the sadness at the passing of time, there's joy at witnessing the people our children are becoming. I expect my kids to flourish and amaze me at what they learn and can do on their own. But while I'm celebrating the growth of my children, I am often caught off guard and saddened by the passing of time on *me*, the growth and change and loss I'm experiencing.

The gray hairs that pop throughout my hair. The creaks and pains that come while chasing and playing with the kids. The medical tests and preventative care that must be addressed. Looking at peers and seeing their age spots and changes. The death of friends and medical emergencies. And then there are my hands.

A common refrain I hear from my mother revolves around her hands. "Look at my hands," she says as she grabs her wrinkly skin laughing to mask the sadness and disbelief. "These look like my mother's old hands. I can't believe they're mine."

Yet, my mother's hands don't look that old to me. I see her hands as a witness to her work throughout the years as a teacher and a mother. I picture her days as a teacher with chalk on her hands from a day of notes on the board, pens marking assignments, the endless filing of paperwork, and the gentle touch on a student's shoulder.

Now, as a mother myself, I walk with my children and hear my daughter's voice: "Hold my hand, Mama." My daughter extends her hand, and our fingers entwine and swing together back and forth. Between my daughter's newly painted pink nails I see my dry, cracked nails and winter's grip taking the moisture from my hands. There are sun spots and blemishes I hadn't noticed before, a roughness in contrast to my daughter's youth. All of a sudden I hear my mother's voice: "I can't believe these are my hands." Her words are now mine. I wonder how my hands have aged so much.

Is it so bad to have these hands? Is it something to turn away from, this aging, this changing of our bodies? I hope not, but it's hard not to lament the people we were and the youthfulness we once felt.

Holding the hands of my children I see a flash of images: reaching to hold my babies for the first time, cradling a newborn in the stillness of the night, learning to swaddle, endless diaper changes, small fingers curling around mine, catching a toddler at the base of a slide, chopping veggies, building forts, piecing puzzles together, coloring, turning page after page of books, packing lunches, folding blankets over sleeping children. My hands have rubbed, massaged, bandaged, cleaned, and loved.

My hands have been embraced and have embraced. And that's where I stop lamenting and turn to gratitude.

Whether we're excited to enter new decades or worried about how our bodies will change, we can continue to lift up prayers of gratitude. Look at your hands and offer a prayer of thanks for all that they have carried since becoming a mother. Turn to this moment and see your hands, your body, and the life you've been given, and give thanks to God.

PRACTICE

Find pictures of your parents or caregivers. Share with your children your memories of growing up and all the ways your family supported and loved you. Give thanks to the God who knit you and your family together. Remember the strength and beauty of the bodies who have held and cared for you.

PRAYER

God who knew me before I was born and has been with me ever since, thank you. Help me to appreciate the gift of my body; this body that has held and cared and picked up children. This body that has sustained me and my babies. This body that is finite and achy and graying. May I commit to hearing these words: *My body is a gift. My body is beautiful.* Amen.

THE POWER OF WORDS
LEARNING GENEROSITY
FROM OUR CHILDREN

Erin

You will be enriched in every way for your great generosity.

–2 Corinthians 9:11

very year since Jack turned one, we've made valentines for his grandparents and godparents. Red and pink construction paper, a pile of crayons, scissors, and stickers go in the middle of the dining room table, then we get to work. I cut out hearts and craft messages, then pass each valentine to him for decoration.

At four, Jack adds bold scribbles and a smattering of stickers to the heart cut-outs, but he's not quite ready to sign his name. I sign for him, imagining the day when he'll be old enough to do it himself, perhaps adding a special greeting.

"Who is this one for, Mommy?" he asks, holding up a pink heart.

"Well, that one is for Great-Grandma, and this red one is for Uncle Andrew's family," I start, rattling off the names on our list. We've kept the list small, simply because we both have a limited amount of endurance for these sorts of projects. Though I prefer digital communication, I know how much snail mail means to our family, especially those who live far away.

After the valentines are finished, I stuff each into a hand-addressed envelope along with a special Bible verse I've chosen for the recipients. What I hope my son learns from this tradition is that words can warm another's heart. In a world where words are often used to chide, condemn, and coerce, I want him to know every word counts, and we can use ours to foster happiness, comfort, and care.

As I seal each envelope and add it to the stack, I say a silent, simple prayer for its recipients—that they may feel seen and loved when they open their valentine. When we've made it through our list, I start packing up the craft supplies, declaring that we're finished.

"Mommy," Jack asks, looking up at me with wide blue eyes, "Can we make a card for Peg?"

Peg is our elderly next-door neighbor. To be honest, I hadn't even thought of her. The fact that Jack does makes me beam with pride.

"Of course!" I say, patting his shoulder. "Thank you for thinking of her, buddy."

Cutting out a new heart, I think, I want to love like this—fiercely and broadly, seeing those who are often forgotten, using my gifts to make others feel seen and known.

PRACTICE

Is there someone in your neighborhood or church who could use a reminder that they are beloved children of God? How might you and your children offer them words from your heart? God delights in us when we share with our neighbors.

PRAYER

Loving God,
you sent us the Word
to live among us,
to save us
and show us the meaning
of unconditional love.
Let my words
be a beacon
reflecting
God's goodness
and grace.
Amen.

MORE THAN A MESS
SEASONS OF PAYING ATTENTION

Kim

Arise, shine; for your light has come, and the glory of the LORD has
risen upon you.

–Isaiah 60:1

Scraps of paper litter our house: on the table, scattered on the floor, strewn
about the couch. If there's an open space, you'll probably find cut-up
paper. Both my kids love to draw and write. Charlotte practices writing
the names of her friends. Other times she's making rainbows, ice cream cones, and
hearts for friends and family. She cuts, colors, writes. Repeat.

Isaac too has started drawing pictures of boats, cars, and his family. One
picture had a head with arms and legs sticking out (that would be Charlotte) and a thought bubble coming out of her head with a stick figure of
himself. "That's Charlotte thinking of me while she's at school," he tells us,
matter-of-factly.

I'm not going to lie, the paper makes a mess. Before every meal there's
paper to pile up (or recycle), and anytime we want to sit on the couch, we're
moving paper to clear a space. Small scraps cling to the floor and our clothes.
As soon as we hang up our favorite creations and recycle the other papers, I
watch the kids grab a fresh sheet and start drawing.

Yet, I see something more than just a mess. As a lover of words, art, and
creativity, I love seeing my kids' creations. If I look closely, I see their person-
ality and heart emerging—one word and picture, one line and color combi-
nation, at a time. Their artwork paints a picture of what they like and how
they see the world. We get a glimpse of creation at its finest—honest, playful,
hopeful; gifts offered to the world.

My kids show me over and over the joy found in creating and sharing our
hearts with others. For them, creating is an act of love. "Look, Mama," they
tell me. Behind their words I hear: *I love you and I love showing you the way I*

see the world. Their world complete with trains and scraps of paper and hearts. Watching them create without inhibition, I'm reminded of how powerful it is to bear witness to imagination. And that when we create, we're bringing beauty and hope into the world.

I wonder: could this be how God shows us beauty and love? Are there pieces of art scattered throughout our days which the creator uses to grab our attention? God created for us a tree of orange and red, a neighbor offering fresh baked bread, a child's hand reaching out to be held, churches singing together, friends raising their voices in prayer. When we open our eyes to the life in front of us, can we see the ways God shows up? So often I'd rather pile my children's artwork and put it out of sight, but I realize that's missing the point. Their artwork is a part of our lives, it's joy and beauty and wonder and creativity. It's love splashed and splattered on canvas. It's God's children delighting in this wondrous and vibrant world.

As you walk through your days, some with heartache and uncertainty, keep searching for beauty and hope. Watch God show up in the canvas of your days: in artwork from your children, a friend reaching out, a hot cup of coffee, a homemade meal, the morning sun.

TO PONDER

What makes up the canvas of your days? Keep your eyes open to the beauty before you and say a prayer of thanks for God's new mercies every day.

PRAYER

Beautiful savior, keep my eyes open to your majesty—
may I look up at the blue sky,
may I feel the gentle tap of water against our feet,
may I recognize the different shades of flowers,
may I notice the crinkle in our children's noses,
may I delight in misspelled words and drawings of ice cream.
And in every moment, train my heart to give thanks.
Amen.

A Sledding Date to Remember
The Power of Play

Erin

Let everything that breathes praise the LORD! Praise the LORD!

—Psalm 150:6

onfession: I don't always enjoy playing with my children. This feels difficult to admit because I'm the daughter of a playful mom. You might even say a professional player, given her decades-long career as an elementary school gym teacher. But me? Well, my default mode is getting stuff done. I prefer planning a party over pretend play, snuggling with a book over chasing my child at the playground.

Despite all this, I do my best to set aside my work and lean into play because I've seen how much it means to my children. We've blasted off to outer space from the snug corners of Jack's closet. We've cooked side-by-side in a miniature plastic kitchen and built the tallest Magna-Tile towers ever. We've had sword fights and laundry fights and mixed a bubbling wizard's brew.

One January when Jack was three, he kept requesting to go sledding together after I picked him up from preschool. "Not today," I'd say, and then he pressed me as to why. I replied with a host of reasons: the weather was too cold, I had a few more work emails to complete when we got home, and then I had to cook dinner. And while those things were true, I suspect that my refusal also stemmed from my resistance to play. Perhaps I feel this way because somewhere I internalized the idea that play is a luxury I can't enjoy until it's earned.

Later that month, I was on the way home from dropping my son at preschool. I looked out my window at the sugary white snow blanketing a local park. Ambling up a hill were a dad and his children, all dressed in warm clothes and carrying bright sledding saucers. I instantly felt jealous. How lucky they can do that on a Tuesday morning. I had no idea what this dad did for work or if he stayed home with his kids, but I often felt that, as a working mom, I missed out on some of these opportunities with my children. Yet, here was this dad making an ordinary day extraordinary. Couldn't I do that too?

Sometimes it can seem like there's no time to play alongside our kids, given the myriad responsibilities of adulthood. Or maybe, like me, you don't feel naturally inclined to playfulness. Play is something we often let go as we grow older, but this dad showed me what it could mean to pursue play on this snowy day as well.

That evening, I closed my work inbox early, dressed in my heaviest coat and gloves, and threw Jack's sled in the trunk before I left for daycare pick up. Upon arrival I clasped Jack's hand and told him "I have a surprise for you." I smiled mischievously. "We're going sledding by the old schoolhouse!"

He squealed.

The sledding hill teemed with children. Jack and I dragged his sled across the perfect white snow and positioned ourselves at the top of the crest. "Ready?" I asked, looking over at him.

He sat in his blue sled and nodded. "Mommy, push me!"

With one push, he flew down the hill, giggling all the way.

"Let's do that again!" he cried. "Will you ride with me, Mommy?"

"Oh, I don't know about that," I stammered. Then I remembered my own mother, the professional player. "Okay, let's do it," I said.

Up and down the hill we slipped and sled, smiling and laughing. Rosy circles bloomed against Jack's cheeks, and snow caked our boots and mittens.

When the church bells chimed at 6 p.m., I glanced at the horizon and gasped. Tangerine and hot pink and amber light leapt out of the darkened forest and coated the sledding hill with a honeyed glow. It seemed the whole world was alive, praising.

I turned to my son. Jack stood still, his eyes pointed toward the sunset. Thank you God for this beautiful day, for the gift of play, I prayed silently. For the chance to move our bodies and feel the cold air and revel in the gift of each other.

Time flies, the adage tells us, but now and then it stills and we witness the stunning beauty of our children. Like a mother eager to surprise her children, God offers us glimmers of grace hidden in ordinary moments. But we must be willing to slow down and see.

"Buddy, it's time to go home for dinner," I said to Jack after a few moments.

"One more ride?" he asked, his voice hopeful.

"Yes!" I replied, turning back toward the hill. We raced to the top and sailed down on our sled. And all of it, the snow, the sunset, the play—was worship.

PRACTICE

Surprise your children with a spontaneous playdate. Visit a new playground or go to a children's museum. Bring home new craft supplies or bust out a new bottle of bubbles. Offer your whole self to them and experience the joy of play.

PRAYER

Thank you, God, for play—
for Duplos and stuffies,
sleds and kiddie pools,
craft projects and dress up clothes,
for my children, who invite me to delight
in your wondrous creation.
Amen.

NOTHING IS LOST
SEASONS OF SMALL THINGS

Kim

When they were satisfied, he told his disciples, "Gather up the fragments left over, so that nothing may be lost."

—John 6:12

Once you hear some Bible stories told in a certain way, during a certain period of your life, you can never go back to how you thought before. I vividly remember listening to a preacher reflect on John's account of the Feeding of the 5,000. I especially love this version where it's a little boy who brings fish and bread to Jesus. "There is a boy here who has five barley loaves and two fish. But what are they among so many people?" (John 6:9)

Years ago when I heard this preacher offer her thoughts on this text she talked about her experience of feeling like that little boy. She doubted her gifts. She didn't feel like she was good enough, or knew enough. Yet, this text showed her that all she had to do was show up with what little she had and offer it to God. And then, God acts. We see this small offering from one boy and witness Jesus turn bread and fish into an abundance.

The miracle continues as Jesus not only feeds the people present, but collects the remaining pieces so that nothing would be wasted. Thanks to the preacher's own reflection on this text I was able, too, to see myself as that little boy. I was reminded to trust that what I bring forward into the world will be used by God, and multiplied into more than I could ever do on my own.

There are so many small gifts that we can offer—a kind word, a listening ear, a handwritten note, an invitation to a meal, a prayer, our presence.

As a mother to two small children, it's often the small things that weigh me down: dishes, meals, helping kids get dressed and use the bathroom, picking up toys, playing catch, reading books, coloring together, building with blocks, and listening to stories over and over. It can seem that these tasks are just that, tasks and checklists that need to get done. Yet, if I take the time to listen and invest in the moment, I find an abundance of grace and gifts. I see God at work in transforming what I have to offer into an abundance. I see repeatedly that I am enough, that the work I do for my children and family is enough, and that God is with me in the days of small things. Some days it's the leftovers in the fridge feeding us dinner, the "How are you?" asked to our neighbor that turns into a deeper conversation, the moments on the porch watching the hummingbirds, or the final moments laying with the kids at bedtime.

The little boy teaches that everything we do is a gift given to God. In our sleep deprivation, in our uncertainty, in our worries and anxiety, in our doubts and second guessing, in our comparison to others, we still have something to offer. Our lives and voices are gifts that with God can be transformed to bring healing and hope to our families and our communities.

Maybe you're wondering what small gifts you have to give, or perhaps you're overwhelmed with the tasks to get through each day. "Nothing may be lost," Jesus says to the disciples and to us. Nothing is lost on God. Whatever small things you're doing, know that God sees you. Be assured that you are enough.

PRACTICE

Today, look for the small things of your day—calling a friend, feeding your family, listening to a colleague, volunteering, sending cards to teachers and health care workers—and watch how God turns those small acts into an abundance for God's people.

PRAYER

God of loaves and fishes
God of the hungry and the satisfied
fill me with your love.
Show me how to open my hands
and offer my gifts to others
to see the blessings transform
before my eyes

and to trust that what I put forward
is good and holy and enough.
In Jesus' name I pray.
Amen.

Waiting on a Miracle

Seasons of Trying
to Conceive

Erin

> But those who wait for the LORD shall renew their strength, they
> shall mount up with wings like eagles, they shall run and not be
> weary, they shall walk and not faint.
>
> —Isaiah 40:31

My period was a day late. The telltale symptoms had surfaced: fatigue, bloating, and a jumpy stomach. *Could I be pregnant?* I wondered. My husband Jay and I had been trying to conceive for months.

Within three minutes, the pregnancy test I took revealed the truth: *not pregnant.*

I stared at the test in disbelief, then slammed it into the garbage. Several of my friends and acquaintances were pregnant—some with their third child. We only had one child, but I wished we had a second. I'd choked back tears when, in the span of a week, my best friend from college and my workout buddy told me they were expecting their second babies. Not me. I wasn't expecting again, and the revelation made me want to crawl back under the covers and wallow.

Later that day, I relayed the news to my husband while we cleaned up from dinner. Our son Jack was in the living room, watching *Lilo and Stitch*, out of earshot.

"What if we can't get pregnant?" I said, scraping unfinished pasta from a dish into the garbage. "Jack keeps asking for a little brother."

Jay rinsed a glass in a stream of water before he answered. "I'm happy with our family the way it is," he said. "If it doesn't happen, Jack will be fine." He turned to look at me. "We will, too."

I didn't feel fine. At 34, I didn't want to waste any more time trying to conceive, but we were halfway through the year, and I was not pregnant. I imagined my dream of a second child slipping away like fine sand in an hourglass.

I leaned my hip against the counter and stared at a sunbeam striping across the hardwood floor. *Why isn't this working, God?* I thought. *I'm almost 35, and I'm worried that Jack's going to be an only child. Would you give us another baby?*

Have you asked this question before? No matter your age or how many children you already have, trying to conceive is a delicate season for many moms. Whether we're tracking our cycle with an app or receiving professional fertility treatments, the process stretches us physically, mentally, and spiritually. One day we feel high and hopeful, the next we can crash with sorrow.

While we wait for a baby, we may compare ourselves to other mothers who seemingly had no problems getting pregnant. We agonize and search for answers. During such a time, it may even feel like God is far from us, or silent. We may feel very alone.

But we are not alone. We are in good company with other modern families and with our biblical ancestors who longed for children, but struggled to conceive. Elizabeth and Zechariah clung to their faith after many years of infertility. Then, in their old age, Elizabeth and Zechariah conceived a child, John, who would go on to baptize Jesus. All that time, God had a special plan for their family.

Back in the kitchen, I wiped tears away from my cheeks and responded to my husband's kindness, "You're right, but that doesn't make this any less hard." He stopped washing dishes and wrapped his arms around my shoulders. There we stood, wrapped in an embrace, looking out toward the sun.

If you're still waiting on a miracle, trust that God is with you. Put your hope in the Lord; remember you're not alone. In your hurting and your questions, God is there. In your hoping and your dreaming, God is there. In your praying and your embracing, God is there.

PRACTICE

Find a Bible verse to memorize and turn to in moments where your patience for the desires of your heart runs dry. Try Deuteronomy 7:9, Exodus 14:14, 1 Peter 5:7, or John 3:16.

PRAYER

Omniscient God,
You know the deep ache I feel for another baby.
I'll admit the waiting is getting to me—
the negative pregnancy tests,
the jealousy and heartache,
the sense that time is running out.
In this season of waiting,
wake me up to your presence.
You meet me in the hard spaces
and offer hope.
You take my tired body and raise
it up on eagles' wings.
Amen.

Hand-Me-Down Love
Connection with Others

Kim

For in Christ Jesus you are all children of God through faith. As many of you as were baptized into Christ have clothed yourselves with Christ.

—Galatians 3:26-27

pull Charlotte's yellow comforter back to reveal Elsa and Anna sheets and hear Charlotte's voice, "Tuck me in, Mama." Hopping into bed, she fluffs the pillow and makes sure her head will rest on Elsa. These are her favorite sheets as is anything from Disney's *Frozen* movie, but they're also my favorite sheets, too. Not for their comfort or design, but because of the hands that passed them down to us.

As a toddler, Charlotte received these sheets along with a package of other hand-me-down clothes from a friend who lives states away. My friend's daughter is a few years older than Charlotte, so a couple times a year, we receive a box full of clothes. Our children have only met a handful of times, but I feel like they know each other from the pajamas and coats that are passed between them. From the t-shirts and comfy pants, we know favorite characters and colors. We see the progression of growth as the months pass. And most importantly, we feel their love with every hand-me-down.

I love hand-me-downs and picturing the other kids in the clothes, knowing someone else played, laughed, learned, and made mistakes in the same shirt and pants; knowing other children were wrapped in their parent's embrace. If the clothes could talk, I'd hear them sharing adventures of reaching into the cookie jar, walking neighborhood streets, and playdates at the park. The clothes would tell stories and remind us that in every washing and putting on again, we're pure gifts given freely and shared in love.

Our children put on tank tops and jeans passed down from family to family, and tucked in each shirt pocket and striped pajama shirt, we find the reminder that God clothes us through relationships. The raincoats and sweaters handed down to our kids are tangible reminders that we don't have to go at it alone; we are meant and designed to be drawn together. We all fit together. Soon enough, my kids will outgrow these winter gloves and hats and we will pass them along to another family. I love seeing this image of how communities clothe and care for one another. In footed duck pajamas, a purple hat, and sequined skirts, God's presence is made known.

God clothes us with love when we wrap our children in the hooded frog towel from the neighbor down the street. God clothes us with love when we unpack a box of princess and dinosaur t-shirts from cousins states away. God clothes us with love when we fall asleep at night tucked into Elsa sheets and blankets from friends we see a few times a year.

Next time you dress your children in hand-me-down clothes, picture God wrapping arms of love around you and your children.

PRACTICE

Are there clothes your children are no longer wearing? Take time to give thanks for the places, experiences, and memories with those items. Find someone to gift your hand-me-downs and include a written prayer for the family and a note with the reminder of God's love surrounding them.

PRAYER

For baseball caps and swim hats
matching onesies and swaddle blankets
Mickey tees and princess dresses
I give thanks.
For friends and family who share clothes
and the stories tucked into pockets and sleeves
for the joy of a package of hand-me-downs
I give thanks.
Wrap me in your love, Lord,

and fill me with the knowledge
I am never out of your reach
swaddled and cradled and held
in your presence and grace.
Amen.

WHEN GRIEF SPEAKS
LOSS/MISCARRIAGE

Erin

When you pass through the waters, I will be with you.

—Isaiah 43:2

My thoughts kept circling back to the OB appointment, to the moment my doctor had told me my baby had no heartbeat. She said I'd miscarried at seven weeks, and my uterus was swimming in blood. She said she was so sorry for our loss and asked if I had any breakthrough bleeding. I shook my head no. She said we would make a plan for my care in the appointment room. And when my doctor finally exited the room, I collapsed in the arms of my husband.

"Babe, I'm so sorry," he choked out. The tears came quickly, so hard I could barely catch my breath. After we left that dark room, the bright lights and the cheery flowers on the office walls overwhelmed me. The sweet baby we'd hoped and prayed for had died. I'd been pregnant for a mere seven weeks, and now I was not. My whole body shook as I walked down the hallway. Grief enveloped me.

Afterwards, I texted my friends and asked them to pray for me, because the only prayer on my lips was *Why God?* I felt like I was being punished, I felt like I'd never not be grieving, I didn't know how the pain would go away: I held my head in my hands and struggled to make sense of the loss. Yet, I clung to the promise that God was with me, and that God saw my pain and loss, and held me.

In the days that followed, grief became my constant companion. At breakfast time, I served Jack his cereal but I could not bring my own spoon to my lips. While I drove him to and from preschool, tears trickled down my cheeks, and I struggled to make conversation. Reading him bedtime stories, my voice caught in my throat.

Grief interrupted me, again and again. But somewhere in the middle of the interruptions, I stopped fighting and let my grief speak to me. I don't know when it happened. Only that she spoke. *That was your baby,* she whispered. *You can rest if you need to. You can cry if you want to.* She led me out of the darkness toward hope.

Whatever you're grieving, whatever you're longing for, God knows and hears your cries. Let your grief speak—God is listening.

TO PONDER

Child of God, take a moment to acknowledge loss in your motherhood journey. Know that God can handle your sorrow, doubts, and questions, and God has not forgotten you or your children.

PRAYER

Shock
sorrow
tears
questions
body's betrayal
"quick
surgery"
lasting
heartache.
Womb
tender,
God
remembers.
Amen.

THE WEIGHT OF WORRY
SEASONS OF DOUBT

Kim

But immediately Jesus spoke to them and said, "Take heart, it is I; do not be afraid."

Peter answered him, "LORD, if it is you, command me to come to you on the water." He said, "Come." So Peter got out of the boat, started walking on the water, and came toward Jesus. But when he noticed the strong wind, he became frightened, and beginning to sink, he cried out, "LORD, save me!"

—Matthew 14: 27-30

Over dinner our tradition includes reading a Bible story from one of our children's Bibles. Night after night we keep company with the disciples, walk with Jesus, wonder at creation, and revel in the gift of God's love for all people throughout time and place. I flip through the pages until the kids tell me to stop and read. We let the words of the stories seep into our bodies and minds.

Tonight we read the story of Jesus walking on water and Peter's desire to join him. I know the story. I've preached on it countless times. But tonight the story comes to me after more news of violence and war, and meets me in the worries and anxieties I have for raising my children.

The story begins on water. At first the disciples are afraid of what and who they see coming towards them. A ghost? No, it's Jesus; the One who uses whatever means possible to get to his disciples. His first words remind them to not be afraid. *But I'm afraid, Lord. It feels like my boat is sinking. The storms are raging. The world is on fire. I want to protect and care for my children. I want them to be safe.*

There's something about Jesus that draws Peter closer to the water, closer to being with Jesus. He wants to walk on water, too. If only he can keep his eyes on Jesus. Peter takes a few steps. He walks on water. He's doing it. And then something shifts and changes. He feels the wind and fears for his life. His eyes dart from Jesus to the water, or perhaps up to the skies, or out to the vastness of sea surrounding him. Whatever it was and whatever happened, his eyes fall away from Jesus and his body sinks into the water.

We may be like Peter wanting to walk on water, desiring to reach out and be with Jesus, but losing our balance when something knocks us down. There's the desire for another child and endless negative tests, a diagnosis out of the blue, the loss of income, a broken relationship, fatigue at another day of dishes, diapers, and doling out snacks, a milestone not met, and a world at war.

Some days we feel like this—sinking, drowning, crying out in fear and worry and sadness. Some days we are overcome with grief and raging at the storms surrounding our children and our world. We keep falling deeper and deeper, uncertain of which way is up and how to move forward; afraid to move forward. Nothing seems good enough. The challenges are insurmountable.

Yet, this story tells us that Jesus immediately reaches out to Peter. Immediately he catches him. Immediately Peter is not alone. Jesus meets us in the sinking, always reaching his arms to us. Even in our drowning, we're not alone. As we cry out, "Come, Lord Jesus" and "Why, Lord, why?" Jesus is there in the water telling us he believes in the power to save ourselves, and along with it, our world.

PRACTICE

Make a list of all the things that are weighing you down. Sit with the fear and anxiety. When you are ready, offer them all to Jesus and picture him saying to you, "Don't be afraid, I am with you."

PRAYER

God of comfort, be with me. Hold me as I cry. Calm my nerves. Guide me into your peace. Forever call to me and reach your arms as I fall. Your presence is my strength. In Jesus' name, I pray. Amen.

HOPE IN FLOWERS
PREGNANCY AFTER LOSS

Erin

Consider the lilies, how they grow: they neither toil nor spin; yet
I tell you, even Solomon in all his glory was not clothed like one
of these. But if God so clothes the grass of the field, which is alive
today and tomorrow is thrown into the oven, how much more will
he clothe you—you of little faith!.

–Luke 12:27-28

The first to sprout from the hardened earth were my sunny daffodils.
Mauve hellebores followed, then lavender catmint and pink wildflowers. That spring I often wiped away tears, marveling at their beauty. I
had just miscarried, and it seemed all of creation was blossoming and praising
God—except for me.

After my D&C surgery, I sobbed and sobbed, asking, *God, why did this
happen?* We'd been waiting and trying for years for a second child—I desperately wanted that baby. I know God doesn't cause bad things to happen, but I
raged at God anyway. And though I clung to the belief that my baby was with
God, I couldn't get over the fact that I would never hold my baby in my arms.
At least, not on this side of heaven.

While I grieved, the inside of our home surged with color, too. Loved ones
sent a bright burst of tulips, a spray of spring blooms, a dozen red roses alongside their sympathies. These flowers, picked out especially for me, provided
comfort. They reminded me that, even in the midst of deep grief, I was not
alone, nor was my sweet baby. The beauty showed me I could trust in God's
faithfulness and in the hope of new life through Jesus. I could hold sadness and
hope alongside one another. I could trust my capacity to bloom again.

Now it's summer, and those spring flowers have withered. Two
months have passed since my miscarriage. Today my flowerbeds shine with
cantaloupe-colored daylilies. Butterflies pirouette among the flowers' faces.

Bees hum while collecting pollen. And I am also humming because a tiny baby is growing inside me again. With each subtle shift in my body, I feel like Mary once did—amazed and terrified. The twin prayer on my lips is *Thank you. Help me.*

Tomorrow, I think I will pick a bouquet of our creamy, full hydrangeas to set in a vase on my desk. To remind me to trust in the Master Gardener. To remind me of my tiny miracle.

TO PONDER

What are you grieving today? Where have you noticed new life in your mothering journey? Know that God walks with you in sorrow and joy, and it's okay to feel both emotions alongside each other. Today, be on the lookout for signs of hope.

PRAYER

Creator-God,

You whisper in zephyrs, rustling through lush plants:
Beloved mama, I am with you.

You paint beauty in flower beds, fields, and forests, to announce:
See, I make everything new.

You stitch sunlight among shadows like delicate lace, to remind:
I'll draw near to you, even when you are scared or in pain.

You burst forth from clouds and declare:
I am the Light of the world
—the one who makes goodness grow.
Hold on to hope; bloom;
trust I am with you and your children always.
Amen.

SUMMER AT THE POOL
REMEMBERING OUR BAPTISMS

Kim

And when Jesus had been baptized, just as he came up from the water, suddenly the heavens were opened to him and he saw the Spirit of God descending like a dove and alighting on him. And a voice from heaven said, "This is my Son, the Beloved, with whom I am well pleased."

—Matthew 3:16-17

When the pool opens for the season, my kids want to be there. Even if it's cloudy and cool, when the pool is open, they are ready to swim. Many years on opening day I stay at the edge and watch the kids come up from the water shivering, but full of joy. After summer school we change into swimsuits, grab towels and snacks, and head to the town pool. We meet our friends and always make new ones.

I hold friends' babies so they can change a diaper or wrangle their toddler into the water. We share snacks. We rock each other's sun-drenched babies as they sleep. Sunscreen is a group commodity. We've celebrated birthdays with cupcakes and popsicles. At times it's hard to tell who belongs to whom—we're all looking out for one another's kids.

I witness the passage of time at the pool. When my two children were babies and toddlers, I always held on to them. My legs turned into a speedboat and we'd bump through the water. My hands would hold their bellies while learning to both kick their legs and move their arms. Where Charlotte used to jump into my arms, now I watch her jump hand-in-hand with friends.

At the pool we splash in the water, we let it hold us, going under and coming up; the water is present. Surrounding us. Moving us. Supporting us. We learn to trust our bodies, the strength of our arms, the power of a breath. We feel what it's like to be held and float staring into an endless blue sky. And all along, with each jump and dive and pull with our arms, the water brings us

147

into community. At the pool, summer after summer, I'm attune to remembering our baptisms.

In my Lutheran tradition the water at baptism is generally a splash from the baptismal font. We watch it drip down our foreheads and sometimes startle babies into tears. The water is a gift and a mystery, it's ordinary yet full of God's presence. Water is a tangible, physical sign of God's invisible love. The water is always with us. Baptism claims us as God's children and in that moment with the water and the Word, we are forever declared a loved child of God.

The pool is a great place to remind our children that they are loved just as they are. Each time they splash in the water, we can remind them of the waters of baptism. Each time they stand back afraid, we can declare to them God's presence. Each time they cheer in glee, we can give thanks for God's joy. Each time they share with their friends or work out a disagreement, we acknowledge the body of Christ with us.

Water seems so ordinary, yet our faith teaches us the extraordinary power found in it—through the water and God's Word at our baptism, we are declared good and God's beloved. And every summer, the waters at the pool invite us to splash into this love.

PRACTICE

Get into water as a family. Depending on the weather go outside and splash in a sprinkler, water your plants, or go to a community pool. If you are stuck inside, gather toys for fun in the bathtub, or make a sensory bin with water and toys. Take some water on your finger and mark the sign of the cross on each other's foreheads. Tell each other that you are loved.

PRAYER

God of abundance,
I thank you
for community—
that sees me,
laughs with me,
and celebrates with me.
For friends—

who tend to my kids,
who share snacks,
who delight in one another.
For water—
that splashes and drips over me
and covers me in love.
I celebrate these gifts of your grace
through water and community
trusting I am bound to others
through your love.
Amen.

TELL YOUR STORY
MOTHERHOOD AND IDENTITY

Erin

And remember, I am with you always, to the end of the age.

—Matthew 28:20

When I became a mother, I needed writing because it allowed me to grapple with the giant identity shift happening inside of me. In those early days, I wrote hard and fast, scrawling out ideas in my journal before my son cried for another feeding. Writing my story helped me stitch together the woman I was before giving birth with the mother I was becoming.

Two and a half years later, I sit at a spare desk in our family's dining room, coffee on my left and a ticking clock to the right. The time reads 6:20 a.m. I glance at Jack's door. If I'm lucky, I can eke out 40 minutes of writing before he wakes.

What's different is that this season of motherhood allows me the semblance of a writing routine. A few days a week, whenever everyone is healthy, I rise early to explore ideas and tackle writing assignments. I capture memories with family, and the cascade of emotions I feel on this rollercoaster ride that is motherhood.

On the page I belong to no one but myself. There's no crying to comfort, no milk to fetch, no bottoms to wipe. No texts to return, emails to answer, calls to make. Here I am nothing and I am everything. Line by line, I uncover my vocations—wife, mother, sister, daughter, employee, neighbor, friend, believer.

I need writing like I need oxygen.

What do you need to breathe? What makes you come alive? Trust that you were created in God's image, instilled with unique spiritual gifts to infuse beauty into the world. Maybe you're a storyteller like me. Maybe you have a flair for interior design or throw amazing get-togethers. Maybe you bake fancy cakes or paint with watercolors or sing in your church choir. Maybe you're all those things and more. Your callings beyond motherhood are God-given, holy. A friend and mentor once told me that being called does not always feel easy—some days it feels downright awful. But the alternative—letting my stories go unnamed—feels more unbearable.

Pen to paper, fingers to keyboard, I record, reflect, discover. Motherhood unearthed in me a desire to share my stories, but writing motherhood helps me become a more faith-filled mother. The more I write, the more I see God's story take shape in mine. I'm continually amazed by the grace laced throughout it.

You have a story to share too. Your story before you became a mother has mountaintop moments, peaceful pastures, and deep valleys, each formative in your becoming. And your story with your children is a rich and holy love story, one that's filled with trials, triumphs, delight, and miracles. Through it all God's been active and present, offering you love and care. Write the words of your life and see for yourself.

PRACTICE

What story will you claim today? Pick up your pen, your phone, or your computer. Write what motherhood looks like this season. Tell a secret. Capture something funny. Record an ordinary moment you loved. When you're finished, share your story with someone you love.

PRAYER

Author of all goodness,
sometimes taking time for me can feel hard
but I know that it's good to share my gifts
and when I share my story—your story—
I amplify the impact of your perfect love.
Amen.

Important Work

Seasons of Paying Attention

Kim

> Whatever your task, put yourselves into it, as done for the LORD
> and not for your masters.
>
> —Colossians 3:23

Blocks, cars, Legos, and Barbie shoes take over any open space on my dining and living room floors. When the light hits our wood floors, the colors of the Magna-Tiles scatter across our white walls—a rainbow of light cascading in front of us. One morning, from the kitchen where I'm cleaning up the breakfast dishes, I hear the sliding of tiles and blocks. I peek my head around and see Isaac moving his train. Square and triangle shapes connect with cars and trucks sprinkled everywhere. His plastic farm animals are squeezed into the makeshift train.

Turning back to the breakfast dishes piled in the sink and the sound of brewing coffee, Isaac's voice breaks through, "Coming through, I've got big important things to do."

Water rushes over my hands; the scent of peppermint soap wafts through the air. "Mama, come look, come look!" My shoulders go up with a deep sigh when I glance at the pile of dishes extending down the counter. I check the time and mentally prepare for the lunch time prep. It feels like I can never get a handle on the kitchen work. There's always some pile to put away or some veggies to chop. On top of that, there's always a bathroom to clean, someone to call, or an appointment to make. Motherhood is a list of never-ending tasks and to-do's. There's never enough time.

Isaac keeps yelling for me to come look. Voices imploring "Come look!" permeate our home and yard. Whether it's their latest art creation, a funny picture in the new book, a bug crawling in the grass, or the tower of blocks balancing precariously on top of each other, the kids want me to see what they are doing; how they're moving through the world. I feel guilty for not engaging with Isaac, so I put down the dish I am cleaning and walk back to the dining room. "My animals are going somewhere and the workers are building something," Isaac says.

Do you feel this tension of managing all the things and taking time with your children? Knowing the work that needs done in the home and at the office and the kids who desire attention, how do you choose where to spend your time? Sometimes we have to get the lunches packed and the beds made, but other times we do have space to sit and watch our children. We get to relish in the importance of play and being with our kids.

Isaac turns away from me and back to his important work. I know the dishes are still in the sink and other meals need to be prepped, but I stay and watch him play, listening as he conjures up stories and cities and work. I catch the light dancing on the walls, see the sparkle in his eyes, and for a moment I'm present to the gift of this life—to my son, our love, his playfulness, and the chance to watch it unfold.

There's no rush to do the dishes. This right here is my important work.

PRACTICE

Picture Jesus watching you during the day and imagine his words to you: "You are my important work and I love you." Rest in God's desire for you to know this love and grace, and then share it with someone you love. Give yourself permission to prefer meaningful time spent with family over day-to-day tasks or work.

PRAYER

Dear God,
this is motherhood—
tantrums and hugs
tears and belly laughs
sticky fingers and missing socks
blocks and racecars
dishes and to-do's
feeling lost and feeling found
tossing and turning

wondering and waiting
hoping and praying
believing and doubting.

This is motherhood
this is my life
infused with holiness
dripping with grace.

Open my eyes to the beauty
and the gift
of this moment
right here and right now.
Amen.

How to Listen
Sacred Attention

Erin

Those who are attentive to a matter will prosper,
and happy are those who trust in the LORD.

—Proverbs 16:20

t started, as many great stories do, with the words, "Once upon a time." The first bedtime tale I spun for my son featured his best buddy from school, a magic beanstalk and a castle in the clouds. The next night, I invited Jack to participate: "Tell me," I said, sweeping hair off his forehead, "What did you boys do when you got to the castle?" Jack pondered this for a moment, and made up an answer. Bedtime has never been the same.

Snuggled under his comforter, Jack now asks repeatedly, "Can we tell a bedtime story?" Because I love witnessing his God-given creativity at work, I oblige. My son conjures imaginary treasure hunts, races, rescue missions and more. Some nights, however, I struggle to pay attention. I have half-listened, rushed his stories or worse, tuned him out, wholly absorbed in my thoughts at the end of a long day.

Children are constantly vying for our attention, inviting us to play with or watch them or listen to their long-winded stories. Sometimes, we are so weary from the pressures of grownup life or too buried in our smartphones, we turn down their invitation. What they want most from us, their caretakers, is to be adored.

Like many parents, I want my son to know just how much I care for him. And while it's unrealistic to believe that I can give him 100 percent of my attention every day, I know I can do a better job when I'm presented with an invitation.

In the film *Lady Bird*, the protagonist Christine discusses a paper she wrote about Sacramento. When her teacher, Sister Sarah Joan, compliments her passionate prose, Christine becomes flustered, answering that she simply pays attention.

Sister Sarah Joan suggests that Christine loves Sacramento. Because love and attention are actually the same.

I think Sister Sarah Joan was on to something. If my attention is a form of love, how might I reorient my heart to share this currency with my family? With myself? With Jesus?

I have not mastered listening to my son's bedtime stories, but I will not stop trying. Indeed, when I really listen, I find he tells me the most profound things.

For instance, the other day at bedtime, Jack told me, "I love my Mommy because she is so nice. Mommy is love." For a moment, his words rendered me speechless. Finally, I replied, "Thank you, love," because I think the same of him.

Maybe this is a kind of grace—knowing we won't always get it right but continuing to tend to our children, to delight in their gifts and passions, to be surprised by the force of their love.

TO PONDER

Attending to our children is hard, holy labor. When you're having a difficult day, perhaps feeling drawn away from your children, you might ask yourself: Why is my attention waning? What would help me attend to the gift of this moment? Maybe you're bored, distracted by technology, or simply need some sleep. Maybe there is a deeper issue that you could bring to God for guidance.

PRAYER

God of grace, train my ears to tend to the voices of my children,
train my eyes to spot the sacred in the mundane,
when I can't give my kids all my attention, it may be a sign I need to rest,
and pour life-giving attention into me—
time with the Word and words of prayer,
stillness and quiet, perhaps a meal,
and when I return to mother,

lift my heart and allow me to bear witness to
the miracle of my children, giving them holy attention
as you give to us.
Amen.

"I'm Sorry"

Asking Forgiveness

Kim

If we confess our sins, [God] who is faithful and just will forgive us our sins and cleanse us from all unrighteousness.

—1 John 1:9

With the closing of the front door, the kids kick their shoes off, leaving them scattered on the carpet. I turn to the clock and see it's 8:40 p.m., well past the kids' bedtime. After a night at our church's vacation Bible school, it's time to get teeth brushed and bodies in bed. Dishes are piled in the sink from dinner and the cumulation of nights away from home has toys strewn about and mail stacked on the kitchen table.

"I'm hungry," Isaac whines. Charlotte grabs one of his toys, and he reaches to take it back with a loud, "NO!" Taking a deep breath, I open the fridge and grab the jar of applesauce. The minutes are ticking by and all I want is to rest.

The kids aren't doing anything inherently bad, we're all just tired. My patience is thin after volunteering for a night corralling kindergarteners. Both Charlotte and Isaac are exhausted from the hours playing, singing, and laughing with their friends. I can't get them to bed soon enough, but they're hungry and thirsty. I hear my voice rising, and feel a tightening in my body, as I ask them to come and eat and then put their dishes away and make their way to the bathroom. "It's time for bed," I repeat with increased frequency and loudness.

I know I should be more patient—they can't help that it's been a busy week. But I also can't seem to help my fraying patience. I watch the kids fighting over the same toy, again. This time my voice rises. "Give it back!" I shout.

I immediately watch Charlotte's face turn away and sink down into her chest while Isaac stops playing and stands still. Charlotte then rushes to the couch, flopping head first into the pillows. "Charlotte," I say with a sigh more at myself than anyone else, "I'm sorry I'm getting frustrated, but we all need to get some rest."

Taking a deep breath I sit by Charlotte on the couch. She pushes away from me, but I put my hand on her back. Rubbing her gently, "I'm sorry, Charlotte. Mama is tired, too."

Charlotte heads to the bathroom where I attempt to stay calm to get teeth brushed and pajamas on. As they toss laundry in the basket and snuggle into their blankets, I keep rehearsing my yelling with a growing pit in my stomach.

After multiple good nights and hugs, and with the final check of the monitor, I still feel bad for how my words sounded throughout the night. I know the kids could tell I was tired, but why did I get so frustrated? In my head I go over what was so bad about the night, and why I couldn't keep myself calm. The kids were being kids. Exhaustion took over their bodies. I don't want my kids to only know frustration and tiredness from me. I want them to feel the love I have for them and the joy I experience in being their mother, but tonight, that didn't come through.

If you have moments you would like to do over as a mother, you're not alone. Whether it's yelling, losing your patience, or constantly feeling frustrated at yourself and your kids, the way forward is the same: asking for forgiveness.

"I'm sorry," comes as easily these days as the yelling. We all make mistakes, but I know that in modeling to Charlotte and Isaac what it is to apologize, I'm showing them the range of emotions we all experience. They also see that I, too, need to be forgiven. I need God's grace to rain on me. I need to come before my children and God, humble myself, and offer the words, "I'm sorry."

In the morning, Charlotte runs down the hallway while I'm writing at my desk. She tiptoes into my office, "Good morning, "Charlotte." I turn and open my arms for a hug as she falls into them with a smile. My voice is soft and calm, "I love you." In our embrace I hear God's words fall over me, *I love you. You are forgiven. My mercies are new every day.*

TO PONDER

Is it easy for you to apologize to your family? If not, consider why. Were you raised in an environment where you heard the words, "I'm sorry"? If so, what effect did this have on you?

PRAYER

Forgiving God,
when I feel overwhelmed, give me peace.
When I lose my temper, give me peace.
When I can't stop arguing, give me peace.
When I need rest, give me peace.
Help me to offer forgiveness.
Help me to seek forgiveness.
Trusting, always, your mercy renews me.
In Jesus' name, I pray. Amen.

SAME TEAM
MARRIAGE AND PARENTING TOGETHER

Erin

Two are better than one, because they have a good reward for their toil. For if they fall, one will lift up the other.

–Ecclesiastes 4:9

Jay and I had been fighting a lot. Chief among our disputes was how to guide our five-year-old's behavior. I followed a parenting style that preached honoring emotions over punishments. Jay felt it was time to start enforcing consequences.

"We have no discipline," he'd grumble at difficult parenting junctures.

"Jack needs connection not correction," I'd counter, ad nauseam. We ended up spending more time criticizing each other's approach instead of redirecting our child.

"Are you guys fighting *again*?" Jack asked us one evening, raising his eyebrows.

My cheeks burned. How much of our fighting had he witnessed?

Something had to change. Too many nights I'd gone to bed fuming or tearful or both, praying for our marriage. *Help us, God, I'd plead. Help us get back to the partnership we had before we were parents.* I wanted us to come together. I wanted to have what brought us together in the first place—heartfelt, easy conversations. With a new baby at home, I couldn't remember the last time we'd done that.

After bedtime, Jay and I sat on the playroom floor and spoke honestly and tenderly to each other. We realized we'd been keeping score of each other's past shortcomings, letting resentment build and build until it nearly broke us. Meanwhile, we hadn't figured out how to solve our parenting dilemma.

"I just want to feel like we're on the same team," I told Jay, uncrossing my arms.

161

"So let's start acting like it," he said, reaching for me. "How can we set some boundaries for Jack?"

Since then, "Same team" has become our mantra when we're embroiled in a parenting dilemma. I'll repeat the phrase to my oldest when he says, "Dad says I couldn't, but can I…" Sometimes, being on the same team is a shared glance at the dinner table. Sometimes, it's switching in and caring for our two children when one of us needs to recharge on the bench.

Same team isn't relegated to parenting. It's when Jay makes me coffee after an exhausting night with the baby. Or when I do his laundry because I notice he's running low on underwear. It's him picking up a book of poetry for me and me planning a day date and setting up childcare, even though leaving our work and home feels impossible.

Marriage is a promise two loving adults make before God to cherish and care for one another. If you're married, listen to and build up your spouse. Celebrate their wins, no matter how small. Go to church and pray together. Connect and talk strategies about your family game plan. When you stop keeping score and start encouraging one another, you win big—together.

PRACTICE

Set aside weekly or daily check-in time with your spouse. It doesn't have to be long; start out by committing to 15 minutes. Pour yourselves a cup of cocoa or a glass of wine. Cozy up on the couch together. Start by exchanging important information you need for planning purposes. Then answer these questions with humility and curiosity: Are there aspects of your partnership in which you may feel divided? In what areas do you feel connected? Finally, ask each other how you can be a better teammate to one another and take notes on one another's answers. Commit to making changes to support each other.

PRAYER

Bless our marriage, O God.
Bless our marriage, Jesus.
Bless our marriage, Holy Spirit.

As you work in unity,
may I, too, do the same with my partner
while we raise and love our children.
Amen.

BEFORE YOU WERE BORN
TRUSTING IN GOD

Kim

In the beginning was the Word, and the Word was with God, and the Word was God.

—John 1:1

At the top of the kids' closets, large photo albums line the shelves. Beginning with their first birthday, we've gifted each child a baby book filled with memories and pictures from the year. They pull the books down and flip through the pages smiling and laughing, "Look at me!" Charlotte says. "Here's me sliding down the slide at the park!"

Isaac turns to me and asks, "Where was I?"

Charlotte quickly replies, "You weren't there, just me." "That's right, you weren't born yet," I remind him.

Isaac looks at the picture again and points to my belly, "Was I in your tummy?" "No, buddy, you weren't even in my belly yet." "Then where was I?"

"With God." Charlotte answers.

We have a variation of this conversation most times we flip through their baby books, or if the kids are scrolling through pictures on my phone. They love seeing themselves as younger versions—the clothes they wore, places visited, and surrounded by friends and family. Flipping through their books helps me give thanks for the growth they've experienced, and the lessons I've learned, too, as their mother.

The older my kids get, the harder time I have remembering what they were like as babies and small children. That's why I love looking through pictures and seeing this time-capsule of our lives. Each picture brings a memory and a feeling, and together the kids and I give thanks for the adventures and beauty we've experienced. But this question—"where was I before I was in your belly?"—continues to humble me, and leave me with few words. The answer lies somewhere between faith and doubt, certainty and uncertainty, and what

I hope to be true. Because really, where were we before we were born? Where were any of us? What was creation before God breathed life into the world?

My answer to the kids usually falls back to, "I don't know, but I believe you were with God." The kids ask where they were before they existed in my belly—while I can't answer with certitude, I can tell them that my love for them existed, even before I knew them, even before we were ever pregnant. And so it is with God. I can't know for certain how creation came to be, and truthfully, I'd rather live in the mystery. This beautiful mystery of God's presence in, with, and around us. This beautiful presence of the Lord of all who transcends place and time. This beautiful mystery of the God who loved us into being. And in this love we've always been known, and in the right time, called by the One who breathes life into all creation.

Our children will have more and more questions about God and faith and how to live this life as a follower of Jesus, and we won't know the answers to their wrestling. But we can keep pointing them back to this love of God that formed them. We can continue to trust the mystery of the Creator's presence and surround them in love, the same love that has known us for all time.

TO PONDER

Are there questions your children ask that are hard to answer? What are some of your questions about God? Reflect on the mystery of faith and see how God is meeting you in the questions.

PRAYER

God of all time and of all places, you loved me into being. From the beginning, you were there. From darkness, you created light. From nothing, you brought forth the world. You keep drawing me closer to you. You keep creating from love. Forever and ever, I am yours. Amen.

Prayers While Expecting

Preparing for a New Baby

Erin

[Children] are indeed a heritage from the LORD.

—Psalm 127:3

My task for this weekend is to pack my hospital bag. I've been telling everyone who asks that we have everything we need for our second child, but once I start packing, I realize we're missing some key items from Jack's first year.

I pull up my Target app and start searching for the missing items: one new bottle brush—click. New Lansinoh cream for nursing—click. A soft crib sheet studded with stars, a new nursing cover, extra deodorant for my hospital stay. Click, click, click.

I hit one final click to confirm my purchases and announce to Jay in the kitchen, "That's the last of it!"

"The last of what?" he asks, looking up from the dishes.

"The last of our baby list," I say, striding to the refrigerator to cross "pack hospital bag" off our baby to-do list. "I just need you to pick up this Target order and we'll be set."

"Sure babe," Jay replies, turning a dish over in a stream of water.

"This is exciting! Thank you for all your help," I say, kissing him on the cheek. I turn on my heel and enter our nearby bedroom, which will also serve as a nursery for our newborn. My son's old crib sits against the far wall by the windows. In the corner stands our Maplewood dresser, once covered with picture frames, now decked with a changing pad, baby monitor, and sound machine. My eyes land on our newest addition: a dove gray glider, a gift from Jay to replace the old rocking chair I used to feed Jack. I melt into the glider and issue a little exhale. It is so comfortable.

Just then Jack ambles around the corner and leaps into my lap. "Hey buddy," I say, folding my arms around him and readjusting him so he isn't pressing on my belly. "I was just getting some things ready for little brother. Are you ready to be a big brother?"

"Uh-huh… uh, Mom?" he asks, looking up at me. "Does the baby know how to swim?"

I giggle and pat my stomach. Jack is learning to swim himself and making good progress in his lessons, which must be where this question came from. "Your little brother's swimming in my tummy, I suppose. But can he swim like you in the pool? No. Maybe when he's old enough—closer to your age—you can help teach him?" He nods affirmatively.

Pulling Jack into another hug, I think of the many questions I have for God: Will Jack's little brother arrive on time? Or will he surprise us? Will he be healthy? Or will he experience some complications?

Will he be strong-willed like his brother? Pragmatic like his father? A dreamer like me?

And how will I change? How will I tend it all—two boys, our marriage, my relationships and work? How will I make it through those sleep-scarce nights? How will I make room in my heart for another child?

How will I carry this extra weight? How long can I hold onto this precious gift, really savoring him? How long until I'll have time just for me?

Who will my baby become? What kind of world will he inherit? Can I keep him safe? And if the answer is what I know—not always—can I learn to live in that mystery? Can I cling to the promise of skinned knees and deepening laugh lines, a boy learning to ride his bike alone, sometimes wobbly, sometimes unsure, looking back at me, eventually gaining speed and balance and traveling miles on end on his own?

These are the prayers I offer to God—wonders and worries and a heart full of hope.

TO PONDER

Much of the preparations for a new baby involve sorting through clothes and supplies. But what about our hearts? How do we prepare them for a new child's arrival? Perhaps we begin by asking these very questions, then shift to what we do know about the One who mothers us all. What do we know about God? God loves us dearly, and each child entrusted to us is a miracle from God.

PRAYER

Holy is my womb,
holy is the nest,
may this time of expectation
be richly blessed.
Amen.

GOD REMEMBERS
SEASONS OF PAYING ATTENTION

Kim

> You yourselves are our letter, written on our hearts, to be known and read by all, and you show that you are a letter of Christ, prepared by us, written not with ink but with the Spirit of the living God, not on tablets of stone but on tablets of human hearts. Such is the confidence that we have through Christ toward God.
>
> –2 Corinthians 3:2-4

When my kids started asking over and over to see my phone for pictures and games, I started leaving my phone in another room.

As a writer this often means I commit to memory a scene as it's playing out. I repeat my children's words and the questions they ask. I notice my daughter's curls and the way my son's thumb goes to his mouth. I feel the weight of their bodies pressed next to mine. I smile as they pour flour, butter, and milk into a mixing bowl for bread. I delight in catching them reading quietly by themselves or building a tower of blocks. Many times, I think to myself that I'd like to take a picture to capture this moment in time.

Social media bombards our eyes with posts about birthdays, the big events, and milestones, and if we don't share the picture, we wonder: "Did this even happen?" My version of that question revolves not around whether it happened, but rather, "Will I remember this moment?"

Will I remember the joy I saw on my daughter's face while she was singing about God's light? Will I remember the excitement of my son's voice inviting me to "Come, look!"

Will I remember the helping hands in the garden pulling weeds and finding cucumbers?

Will I remember the moments building blocks and playing with trains?

If there's no picture, will I remember?

When I look at my children, who are now seven and five, I have a hard time remembering what they were like as babies and toddlers. I'm no longer in the season of midnight feedings and endless bottles and diapers. Something new is emerging from the two of them each day: new words and phrases, deeper understanding, richer friendships. You may flip through photo albums and have a hard time remembering the seasons you experienced, too. Perhaps you look at your child walking to school and wonder how they got so grown up. We all want to remember this time raising our children, and the gifts found in our days.

When we bike around town, I trail behind them following their joy. We marvel at the dew on the grass and give thanks for the rain to help our garden. I want to snap pictures of them blazing ahead of me, but my phone lies atop a stack of books in the office. So I focus on the blue skies and warmth of the sun, the kids' energy, their love for one another and the gift of being in the neighborhood, and that, in the moment, is enough.

Perhaps you are accustomed to having your phone with you while playing with your kids. Maybe today is the day to put the phone out of sight, join your children in their activities, and commit to being fully present. Watch your children and soak in their voices, the way they walk through the living room, how they hold their favorite stuffies, and feel their bodies settle into your lap.

Will we remember? I don't know, but thankfully God remembers, and writes these moments in our hearts.

TO PONDER

Think of one recent family memory that brings you joy. Take some time to write about it. Include how you felt, what you heard, and what clothes you were wearing. Use all your senses and describe the scene. Say a prayer of thanks for that one moment.

PRAYER

Dear God, help me to keep my eyes open to your presence. I want to see this world in living color. I want to remember the way the light falls in our home and how my childrens' laughter echoes through the halls. I want to remember the whisper of secrets and how it feels to hold the weight of my children in my lap. Keep me present and marveling at the gifts before me. Amen.

"Another Jesus Story, Please!"

Sharing the Gospel
with Children

Erin

> For God so loved the world that he gave his only Son, so that everyone who believes in him may not perish but may have eternal life.
>
> —John 3:16

M y mother-in-law gave Jack a new children's Bible for his fourth birthday. On the cover, Jesus sits with a child in his lap and at his feet, surrounded by characters from the Old Testament—Adam and Eve, Noah, David and Goliath.

From the reading chair, Jack snuggled his back against my chest and I held the new book open in front of him. We dove into God's Word at the very beginning, whipping our way through Genesis and Exodus. Jack heard tales of creation, destruction, exodus, and epic battles. Every tale—abbreviated and designed for children—bled into the next and left my son eager to read more. Each night we read, I noticed the wider narrative arc of the Bible, an arc of birth and death, hardship and hope, conflict and forgiveness. As I read, I encountered stories of a loving God who would do anything to rescue his lost children. Story after story declared the goodness of our Creator and pointed to the coming of Jesus.

The part of the Bible we loved the most was the New Testament, particularly when Jesus lived and performed miracles. Stories Jack had heard in church and Sunday school came alive on the page: we saw Jesus turn water into wine, heal a blind man's sight, walk on water.

When the clock ticked closer to 8:00 p.m., I'd remind Jack we had five more minutes left to read before it was time to brush our teeth and say good-night. "Another Jesus story, please!" he'd ask sweetly, and so we'd read another and another until our time was up.

Reading this children's Bible with my son illuminated the beauty of the Christian narrative—a sprawling love story between God and God's people. At its midpoint, Jesus joins humanity in our struggles. I think the Jesus stories are favorites because they sparkle with adventure, compassion, hope, and miracles. Jesus' way is the way of healing and transformation.

And Jesus was preaching to me again, too. Through a simple children's Bible, I began seeing his life anew. I'm learning to walk like Jesus, to walk the way of love. I'm learning the power of hope and radical forgiveness. I'm reminded that when Jesus invites children to sit at his feet, he means my son but also me. I am one of God's beloved children.

So I'll keep reading my son another Jesus story, filled with hope that the words of the gospel will seep into our very beings, each story reminding us that God's love is real and God's story with us isn't finished.

PRACTICE

Read a children's Bible with your kids. Together, wonder about your favorite stories. What do they tell you about who God is?

PRAYER

Author of the Word,
you sent your son Jesus to show us the way of love.
Jesus, who loved children best
and spent time with those on society's margins.
Jesus, who cured the blind and broken,
who fed hungry hearts in deed and word,
Jesus, gave his life for us so we might find new life in him.
Amen

"I CAN HEAR YOU!"

LISTENING TO OTHERS

Kim

I believe that I shall see the goodness of the LORD in the land of the living. Wait for the LORD; be strong, and let your heart take courage; wait for the LORD!

—Psalm 27:13-14

The walkie-talkies started out as a gift for Stephen and me. Knowing we love camping and hiking as a family, my mother bought us a set to aid communication and safety. They quickly landed in the hands of our kids. Small enough to fit in a pocket but loud enough to be heard across a room, Charlotte and Isaac delighted in talking to one another. They couldn't quite figure out how to hold the button and talk at the same time so they took turns yelling at each other with the walkie-talkie next to their mouth. Repeatedly their voices shouted: "I can hear you!"

Back and forth they went, "I can hear you," followed by laughter and jumping up and down. They could hear each other, but they weren't really listening. They simply enjoyed saying, "I can hear you," and shouting over one another.

The first time they ran off to hide behind trees to "talk," I laughed and smiled as they kept "hearing" one another. But I also couldn't help but wonder if this is how so many of us are communicating today. There's a lot of information, noise, opinions, worry, and uncertainty vying for our attention and weighing down our hearts. It's hard to hear one another. It's hard to listen. The news cycle bombards us 24/7. The latest parenting hacks can be found while scrolling Instagram and Facebook, and all too often we see curated versions of our friends' lives.

I wonder how often we really hear someone?

I want to listen to others. I want to keep my heart open to the diversity of thoughts and opinions around me. Most importantly, I want to model for my children what it means to listen, really listen, to others. When I look into their eyes, scrunch down on my knees to be at their level, they know they have my full attention, and I hope they know that what they say matters.

Our posture towards our kids sends a message that they are valued; their words are valued. We hope our attention motivates them to offer the same presence to others. When so much feels out of our control, offering ourselves to others with attention and listening ears is a gift we can share. Listening and really hearing what another is saying is a way to practice the presence of God. It's a way to see our creator in our neighbors; a way to bring the reign of Christ here on earth. The more we listen to the people in our families and our communities, the more we can see God's goodness in our midst. Every time showing others, "I can hear you," and that they are valued.

PRACTICE

Take time today to really listen. Whether it's with your kids or coworkers or the cashier at the grocery store, ask a question and listen. Don't think about what you'll say next, but simply offer your presence.

PRAYER

Dear Lord, help me to listen. Help me to be still. Guide me in my conversations and interactions with your people so that I offer myself to them in love and grace. Amen.

Brave and Scared

Milestone: First Day
of Preschool

Erin

I can do all things through him who strengthens me.

–Philippians 4:13

O n his first day of preschool, Jack declares, "I go to school!" after he wakes. He dresses in his new Paw Patrol sweatsuit, I pour us two bowls of Rice Krispies, and we sit at the dining room table, peering out the window. Snow falls lightly, powdering the yard with a bit of sparkle. Suddenly the twinkle in Jack's eyes fades. I ask, "What's wrong, buddy?"

He puts his head down next to the bowl and whimpers, "Sce-rred." Jack's cereal pop-crackle-fizzles and deflates as he ignores it.

"Oh... that's understandable. This is a big change. But remember, your best buddy's in your class, and that will make it much easier."

"And," my husband Jay interjects, sliding me a steaming mug of coffee. "You can't be brave without being scared."

I turn to Jay. Impressed, I mouth, "Where did you hear that?" He shrugs and smiles. Jack lifts his head so his eyes appear to be hovering at the edge of his cereal bowl. "Dad, were you ever scared of school?"

Jay chuckles and leans forward. "All the time, bud. All the time."

I recall times I was scared and brave—working as a lifeguard, going off to college, studying abroad, starting my first job after college, buying our first home, giving birth to Jack and parenting him. In Scripture and throughout history, there's an abundance of God's people who were scared and brave. I think of my ancestors who immigrated to the U.S., my dad who flew Black-hawk helicopters for the Army, my mom who raised us while he served. Surely Jochebed trembled when she placed her precious babe in a raft and floated him

175

down the Nile. She trusted God and God took care of her son Moses, bestow-ing on him an important purpose to free God's people.

I am still thinking of this conversation when Jack and I enter the play lot at his preschool. His feet begin to drag while my hand tugs him onward. "I'm shy," he protests. "I don't wanna go."

"It's okay," I say, squeezing his hand. I wish I had more to say here but the truth is, I'm scared, too. Is he ready for this? Will he be safe here?

Outside the doorway, I crouch down to Jack's level while we wait to go inside. The next words I speak are for me and him: "Remember what Daddy said? You can't be brave without being scared."

"Yeah," he whispers, leaning his head against mine.

"I love you, Jack," I say, kissing his cheek.

"I love you, too, Mommy," he returns, hugging me hard. Motherhood, I think, is a sacred waltz of pulling close and stepping apart, of endings and beginnings, of giving and receiving and trusting that our children, and we, can dance on our own.

This life of faith, too, is a sacred dance of doubt and belief, endings and beginnings, death to our old selves and new life with God. We learn love from the One who first loved us into being, and we can trust God's love strengthens us as we dance into the future.

Jack safely inside his new classroom, I turn toward the car and exhale, my breath swirling and vanishing in the crisp winter air.

PRACTICE

Create a threshold ritual to mark your child's comings and goings to school. Perhaps you have a special phrase you'll say to mark your goodbyes. Maybe you will offer a particular snack on a regular day home from school. Maybe each day you'll draw a heart on your children's hand as a reminder of your love. Something as simple as exchanging "I love you" or "God goes with you" day after day does good work in your heart and the heart of your child. Like-wise expressing your excitement after receiving them home from school could include a special phrase such as "I missed you today" or "I thought about you today."

PRAYER

God, when I send my children into the world, grant me courage. Help them remember my love goes with them; help me remember your love goes with me, too. Amen.

First Day
of Kindergarten
Milestone: Starting Kindergarten

Kim

It is the LORD who goes before you. He will be with you; he will not
fail you or forsake you. Do not fear or be dismayed.

–Deuteronomy 31:8

The night before Charlotte starts kindergarten, I walk the dog to the
school praying for the year ahead. In the ten minutes it takes me
through the darkness with the first stars beginning to shine, I wonder
what I'll say to Charlotte before she enters the building. I've done enough reading and heard from enough friends to have a plethora of meaningful rituals to
mark the start of school. Some contenders include:

Remember who you are and whose you are.
Go with God.
Be kind.
I love you.

I want words that will inspire, comfort, and fill her with joy (or perhaps
just words that will calm my nerves). But nothing seems to fit.

The next day, the sun shines without a cloud in the sky. Charlotte wakes
early and can barely eat her breakfast for the excitement she feels.

I think back to the beginning of the summer and this day seemed so far
off, but here we are going to kindergarten. I flash back through our summer—
afternoons at the pool, books on the couch, walks around the park. I mourn
the loss of time we'll have together with lazy mornings making pancakes and
reading before naps.

Before the walk to school, we snap pictures on our front porch of her backpack swallowing her and her smile as bright as the sun. She stands tall next to her brother and father. On the walk, Charlotte takes the lead while I push Isaac in the stroller. I follow behind and wonder how my daughter became so big carrying her backpack and lunch bag and talking to me about her teacher and new friends.

Cars drive past us and doors open with children waving to their parents before walking into the school. "Can I have a hug?" I ask Charlotte.

Charlotte shakes her head no, too much in a hurry to get inside. I open my arms nonetheless holding them to the air.

"Alright, let's go then," Stephen says and reaches his hand to her. She follows him leaving Isaac and I behind. I see her nearing the door and remember I wanted to say something to her.

I haven't shed any tears yet this morning, but as she walks ahead with her dad, without my final blessing or words of encouragement, my lip starts to quiver. I forgot to offer any words to Charlotte on this first day. I can't even remember what words I said to her last.

I lift my hand for a wave and smile as she walks hand-in-hand with her dad, but their backs are to me.

I remember words. I've been them saying over Charlotte since the day she was born.

Words that end our days in the rocking chair. Words that I've spoken over her thousands of times. Words I hope are soaking into her bones and becoming a part of her. Words I pray will be holding her at school and through her whole life whispering to her over and over: *Remember that you are a loved child of God.*

TO PONDER

Think about the first and last words you say to your children each day. How do you want them to feel when they hear you speak to them? How do you feel when you first greet them in the morning and send them to bed? Next, reflect on words God says to you every day: *you are mine, you are loved, you are called.* Receive these words and trust they are yours.

PRAYER

God of all beginnings and endings, thank you for your presence. Guide me as I step into something new, trusting you go before me, and help me to give thanks for where I have been. May your words be a blanket over me all my days: I am loved, I am loved, I am loved. Amen.

GOODBYE DIAPERS
MILESTONE: MASTERED POTTY-TRAINING

Erin

So teach us to count our days
that we may gain a wise heart.

—Psalm 90:12

My son Jack was three days old the first time I changed his diaper. Jack had arrived fresh from the hospital's NICU after being treated for bilirubin, and I was still scared to hold his fragile body. The sweet-tangy smell of newborn poop shifted the air in my hospital room. My hands shook. I removed the yellow sticky tabs from the newborn diaper circling his warm, soft body. I stopped and looked around the room, wishing someone could swoop in and save me.

Come on, Erin, you can do this. You just did it a month ago on a plastic baby doll at the new parents' class. Standing at the edge of his bassinet, I chuckled at the open diaper. I'd nearly forgotten—they told us newborn poop *was* bright yellow!

Diaper changes got easier as the months went on. My hands became steadier. My son's body began taking up more space on his chevron-striped changing pad. We started buying size 1/2s instead of newborn/1s. The frequency of changes declined yet their contents grew more... dramatic.

Once, during Jack's first year, some friends visited our home with their children. My friend, a veteran mom, impressed me by whipping off and changing her toddler's wet diaper while he was standing in the middle of our living room. My mouth flopped open in surprise. This was next-level parenting!

Months later, my son dropped his middle-of-the-night diaper change and feeding, and I rejoiced. By then, I handled blowouts and routine changes with ease. Later still, when Jack entered the toddler stage, I became the admirable mom at the playdate. I could whip off a wet diaper while he was standing and switch it with a clean one in less than a minute.

Whether my hands shook or felt steady, each diaper change was a sign of my son's growth, and ultimately, of our faithful God who nourished his body.

My son's last day of diapers arrived unbidden. He was four, already potty-trained for over a year, but still wearing nighttime diapers. After a week of waking with dry diapers, I asked Jack if he was ready to sleep in his "big boy underwear." He shouted "Yeah!" with gusto. The following morning he was dry, and we celebrated with a high five. Just like that, we said goodbye to diapers.

In Psalm 90:12 the speaker declares, "So teach us to count our days that we may gain a wise heart." Perhaps it's not what the psalmist intended, but I hear these words and think of diapers. On the hard days in early parenting, I relished the thought of a future free of diaper changes. God's word, however, encourages us to stay present amid goodness and challenge. Change is constant, but those who recognize the blessings in each day are wise.

Later, I held Jack's extra overnight diapers in my hands and blinked back tears. This milestone was a salient reminder of my son's growing independence. I thanked God for Jack's days in diapers that made me a mother. And I grinned at the prospect of our new adventures to come—*sans* diapers.

TO PONDER

Name your season of parenting. Are you still in the diaper days or mastering potty-training? What's hard? What do you love? Is there any aspect from which you may be counting down? How does a sense of the future help you reframe some challenges as moments to cherish?

PRAYER

God of all time, help me know that you are with me during growth and change. Whether my hands shake or feel steady, you are present. Steady me with your love so I feel equipped for this motherhood journey. Encourage me to cherish each transition and allow it to teach me your wisdom. Amen.

A CALENDAR OF PRAYERS
PRACTICING GRATITUDE

Kim

The human mind plans the way, but the LORD directs the steps.

–Proverbs 16:9

A cross from the kitchen sink, the sun's first light lands on a square dry-erase calendar fixed to the wall. Fresh fruit sits in piles, and bright shapes and colors from my children's artwork hang next to it.

When Charlotte started kindergarten, we bought the calendar to show her when she'd have school and to keep track of all her activities. With each diagonal line cut through a completed day, I whisper a silent, "Thank you, God." I'm grateful to experience these days.

Every month she drags a small chair to the calendar, moves the fruit cart, and stands up to reach the wall. "What month, Mama?" she asks me, marker in hand, poised to write.

"June," I tell her. I spell out each letter and pause while she grips the marker, never taking her eyes off the letters. It's this same spot in our kitchen where her baby bottles were assembled, where I rocked her back and forth waiting for the coffee to brew, where I stumbled in moonlight for 3:00 a.m. wake-ups, where I cut her grapes in half for a snack. Her artwork hangs on the wall next to this spot, every color and line a reminder of how much she has grown.

I see the calendar when I grab a banana for our morning smoothie and when I turn off the last kitchen light before bed. It helps me look forward, but also back in time to all the ways we have been together as a family, for all the ways that God has shown up in our lives with grace, love, and forgiveness. Too soon, Charlotte may not have the time or desire to fill out our calendar, and too soon, the calendar will no longer mark my days with small children.

The calendar bears witness to all the ways we spend our days—weekly Friday movie nights, mom meetings and dad meetings, church on Sundays, camping trips, picnics with friends, school days, T-ball games, and birthdays. Each square holds an infinite number of possibilities; we can't fit in all the activities and meals and, most importantly, the love we experience. Each night, I try to remember as much as I can, but often, the days blur together, slipping away from me as easily as we cross them off.

Charlotte loves to count the days and delights in looking ahead to what is to come.

I wonder if God sees the world in this way too: full of potential, hope, and joy. I see the passage of time, how much each one of us has changed, how much I hope to remember, how much I hope to be present, but perhaps God only sees an abundance of riches found in God's beloved children.

TO PONDER

Look at your calendar with all your activities, meetings, and events. Do you notice any patterns? Do you feel overwhelmed or excited for the month ahead? How can you use this knowledge for deepening your relationships and being present throughout your days?

PRAYER

Ever-present God, you invite me to know you and love you throughout my days. Keep me mindful of the gift of this life. Amen.

ROOTED

THE GIFTS OF COMMUNITY

Erin

As you therefore have received Christ Jesus the LORD, continue to
live your lives in him, rooted and built up in him and established in
the faith, just as you were taught, abounding in thanksgiving.

–Colossians 2:6-7

started dreaming of a move in 2020. Under lockdown that spring, our modest Chicago home seemed less charming and more cramped than ever. No longer alone when I worked, I longed for an office of my own instead of a writing desk jammed into the dining room. I wanted a big backyard where our three-year-old could play on a swing set instead of our small patch of grass. Most of all, I wanted another bedroom for the second child for which I'd been praying.

In May of 2021, I became pregnant. Suddenly, the need for a bigger home felt even more urgent. I drew up a list of other places to live and shared it with my husband. We needed what I hoped would become our forever home, the place where we'd finally put down roots.

"We can make this happen," I told Jay, holding out my offering. "Don't you think it's time for our next adventure?"

"I guess," he shrugged, surveying our living room. "I like it here."

"But it's getting too small for our family," I said, gesturing to my expanding belly. "And we're so far from our good friends and parents."

Jay agreed. However, given the challenging housing market, we decided to table our search until the spring of 2022.

As time passed, I found myself pulling back from investing in relationships or my church, telling myself that our future home was where I'd really set down roots. I was in the midst of a difficult pregnancy and fantasizing about another neighborhood felt more comfortable than fully investing in mine.

185

Fast forward to 2022: I gave birth to our second child on a snowy day in February. Friends from our street and beyond came to our icy doorstep bearing chicken chili, blueberry muffins, and vegetarian enchiladas. Gift cards to Target and Grubhub arrived in my email inbox. Online and in real life, neighbors and friends gushed over our newborn.

Their outpouring of love—so unexpected and enthusiastic—brought me to tears. I felt seen in a way I hadn't since before the pandemic, and each small kindness stirred up in me a new set of dreams. The desire I'd had to root once we moved, the dream I had of making close friends once we were settled, the pulling back I'd done under the guise of "Why bother?", until our home fit the perfect vision I had for it? It dissipated.

A new question surfaced: What would it look like to root ourselves now?

Maybe being rooted was less about location and more about connection. The people around us had shown up for us, had gifts to offer us. I didn't want to overlook the relationships God set before us because I was too busy looking ahead at the future. God continually shows up in our lives through the people we meet, and the places we go, it's just a matter of noticing where we are.

There are moments in life when we approach a bend in the road and feel ourselves being pulled to a new path. Job opportunities, expanding our families, caring for aging parents, and school transitions may require big moves. At these junctures, it's tempting to pull ahead and leave the past behind us. But when we do that, we can miss the little graces God's placed in our path. Don't uproot yourself prematurely. Stay present. Trust that God's working in the between spaces, filling them with opportunities for connection, beauty, and delight.

Our new baby is now five months old and we're still living in our small home. I don't know how long we'll be here, but I don't want our family circumstances to hold me back from true fellowship with God's people. I'm learning the perfection I long for in a home isn't real. I want to root down and be faithful to where and to whom God's calling us.

TO PONDER

God's inviting you into the here and now of the life you have with your family. Are there areas in your life where you feel yourself pulling back from sacred community? What's holding you back? Pick one place or relationship in which you'll put down roots this season and watch what sprouts.

PRAYER

Sometimes I think that I live my life waiting
for the good part, believing that once my home
and my kids line up with my perfect vision
then the good part will begin.
But you've planted me here for a reason, God.
Show me the way to live with *your* perfect vision.
Rooted in you, I'm ready to grow.
Amen.

IF YOU SAY SO
SEASONS OF INSECURITY

Kim

> When [Jesus] had finished speaking he said to Simon, "Put out into
> the deep water and let down your nets for a catch." Simon answered,
> "Master, we have worked all night long but have caught nothing. Yet
> if you say so, I will let down the nets."
>
> —Luke 5:4-5

ired fishermen are hungry. They need to catch fish, not only for their
daily food, but for their livelihood. Imagine the weight placed on their
shoulders and the families that are waiting for them back home. Can
you feel their despair?

Perhaps you have your own despair right now—
A recent medical diagnosis
A child being bullied at school
Lack of communication with your partner
Your child failing to gain weight or utter their first word or crawl or walk

Into this desperation, comes Jesus. He meets the fishermen where they
are—somewhere between hope for fish and despair at what hasn't been. Jesus
invites them to do precisely what they've been doing all night. Jesus doesn't offer
any new tip or trick, he simply tells them to let down their nets.

Can you hear Jesus' voice in your life?
Put your nets down, friends
Give me the worries and anxiety
Tell me what's going on
Let me hold your pain with you

I know when I'm tired and frustrated I can have two responses: rage and giving up OR trying anything at all costs knowing there's nothing left to lose.

Simon responds to Jesus by acknowledging what's happened (*we've worked hard all night and haven't caught anything*).

But Simon also trusts the advice of Jesus who stands before him (*But because you say so, I will let down the nets*).

Simon and the others know what will happen when they put down their nets. Nothing.

Yet, Jesus invites them to put down their nets one more time.

I imagine Simon thinking to himself: We've caught nothing. Casting our nets won't work. There are no fish. Trying again is pointless. But because you say so, Jesus, I'll give it a try.

Simon trusts more in Jesus than in the experiences he had the previous night. He trusts the invitation of Jesus more than the lack of fish he's caught. He trusts Jesus because Jesus said so.

Can you listen for Jesus' invitation to put down your nets—and trust?

Can you listen to Jesus and say:

Because you say so I will reach out to the friend who hurt me.

Because you say so I will offer forgiveness.

Because you say so I will make the appointment.

Because you say so I will believe I'm a good mother.

Because you say so I will invite my neighbors into conversation.

Because you say so I will love myself.

Because you say so I will call myself your beloved child.

Because you say so, Jesus, I will listen.

TO PONDER

Do you feel stuck in your parenting? Are you waiting for a response or answer? Picture yourself on the boat with Jesus and listen for his voice inviting you to drop your fear, anxiety, doubt, and insecurity. Hear Jesus' voice and remember his presence.

PRAYER

Dear God, I'm on the shore waiting for you and listening for your voice. But my fear and the worries that tangle my heart are so big. Release me from my doubt and turn my eyes to you. If you say so I will trust my belovedness and your love above all else. Amen.

WE ARE ONE
PRAYER WITH CHILDREN

Erin

Truly I tell you, whoever does not receive the kingdom of God as a little child will never enter it.

–Mark 10:15

arlier this spring, Jack refused to participate in dinnertime prayers. I shouldn't have been surprised by this development—family dinner had been haphazard since the baby arrived. Nevertheless, I wanted to get us back to acknowledging our source of daily bread, so I asked him why he didn't want to pray with us.

"We say a *different* prayer at school," he told me, eyes glinting with defiance.

"Oh" I said, raising my eyebrows at my husband. Jack's Montessori school isn't affiliated with a particular religion. Some teachers are Muslim, other staff and families are Christian and others still are agnostic. Curious, I asked, "Can you teach it to us?"

Jack began to clap. Then he sang about looking around the room and seeing a family. He described his classmates as brothers and sisters—as one. He finished with a word of thanks for the meal.

As my son's voice grew from soft to louder and more confident, I imagined him praying these words alongside classmates and teachers whose beliefs and skin color are both different from and the same as his.

When he finished my husband and I sat quietly, spellbound by the moment. "Wow," I finally breathed. "That was beautiful."

From that night on, we've been integrating Jack's prayer from school into our dinnertime rituals. Thinking about it now brings tears to my eyes as I consider the horrific acts of violence in the news that regularly confront us, many motivated by the sin of racism. It makes me sick to my stomach with rage that we live in a society where such hate exists.

191

I want to raise my children in a place where everyone can grocery shop and drive and worship without fear. Where we realize our daily bread is abundant and share it with others. Where unity isn't a far-fetched dream, it's a reality.

What the children pray is true: We are all God's children; we are one.

May I do all I can to live it.

TO PONDER

The state of the world can bring us to our knees in sadness, wishing we could make it better for our children. When was the first time your child taught you something about faith? What are they teaching you right now? Paying attention to my little hope-bearers reminds me that they have much to teach me about cultivating peace with our neighbors.

PRAYER

God of grace, accompany me now as I aim to raise peaceful children. Guide my words and actions, and teach me to see my neighbors as beloved siblings in your big, beautiful family. Amen.

LET'S GO FOR A WALK

COMMUNITY AND PRAYER

Kim

Happy are those whose strength is in you, in whose heart are the highways to Zion.

—Psalm 84:5

Every spring and summer morning, our neighbors walk by our house on their daily walk. With their arms looped together, the husband and wife stroll by, waving to me on the porch, then turning back to each other. Later I watch two elderly women out for a stroll with the click of a walking stick announcing their presence. A group of moms pushing strollers walk around the park across the street. And then there's the lady with her French bulldog barking at anyone who passes and stopping occasionally to smell the grass and flowers.

I wonder what thoughts and worries each of these people are holding. Has their morning started out in a rush? Did they receive some news that spiraled their day into uncertainty? Perhaps they're getting over sickness and happy to feel the fresh air on their faces. Maybe they use this walking time to pray and give thanks. Possibly this is the only chance they get with their loved ones and friends. I imagine every step they take as an act of hope, moving towards peace and connecting to the world around them.

Walks are also a sacred time for our family. After school and snacks and the tossing of bookbags on the couch, the kids and I take our turn walking the town sidewalks. It's our time now to wave to the widow weeding her garden beds and to listen to the French bulldog bark at us while we pass his home. Our walks are not always calm or quiet, or necessarily reflective. But we continue to put one foot in front of the other. During our walks we declare: we're here and we see you.

Moving our bodies is an act of faith proclaiming that we will go where the road and sidewalks take us, seeing the beauty and brokenness of our community. Our hearts beat announcing we are alive and able to be present to those we know and those we have yet to meet. We step forward together into our communities showing up in the challenges and the joys.

When we walk as a family, we're not concerned about the distance. Instead, we marvel at the chance to listen to the sound of birds, see the different shades of green in the leaves, hear the cadence of conversations, and witness the changing seasons; all of it prayers rising up like incense. All of our walks deepen our connection to God and God's marvelous creation.

When we walk whether alone or with others, prayers can be offered by moving our feet. Walking allows us to practice loving the earth and the people we meet. One foot in front of the other is as holy a response to life as I can imagine.

Every step a prayer—Lord, thank you for these children, keep us safe, open our eyes to your beauty, help us to slow down, teach us to love our neighbors.

Every step a moment of gratitude.

PRACTICE

Take a technology-free walk as a family. Leave your phones home and step outside with hands free and hearts open to listen. Greet your neighbors with intention and see them as God's beloved children and the world around you anew.

PRAYER

I lift up my eyes to the skies—
where does my help come from?

My help comes from the Lord,
creator of sunrises and sunsets
wild bears and lap dogs
cherry trees, dogwoods, and dandelions,
blades of grass and leaves of gold and red.

The Lord will be with you—

walking beside you
listening to your cries
rejoicing in your joy
holding on to hope with you.

The Lord watches over you—
waking and sleeping
playing and resting
learning and working
running and walking
traveling and staying home.

The Lord will not leave you—
whether in sickness or health
belief or doubt
the Lord calls you beloved child;
the Lord will watch over your coming and going
both now and forever more. Amen.
(Based on Psalm 121)

From First Steps to Biking

Movement Milestones

Erin

For we walk by faith, not by sight.

–2 Corinthians 5:7

One year old

The day my son learns to walk, my husband Jay and I are sitting in the living room. Light streams through the windows. Jack plays on the carpet in front of us, content with his blocks on the coffee table. He's balancing himself on the table when, suddenly, he lets go. Arms pointing toward me, he puts one shaky foot forward, then the other. He lifts his eyes and smiles, toddling forward with a rush of momentum. He toddles right into the couch and I wrap my arms around him and begin to giggle. As a working mom, I missed many milestones during the first year while my son was in daycare. But I didn't miss this one. Thank God I witnessed it. "Oh my GOSH!" I gush. "Jack, you did it!"

Three years old

After dinner, Jay strums his guitar, running through favorite melodies. Jay's playing the song "Everlong" softly when Jack calls, "Mommy, let's dance!"

I grasp his hands and we spin around the living room, smiling at each other. Then I sweep him into my arms and we keep twirling. Jay's still strumming and I hold our son in my arms and think, *This is my life, slow and simple, pure and happy. This life is more beautiful than I could ever imagine. Thank you, thank you, thank you.*

"Mommy, it's very dizzy!" Jack says, so I stop spinning and we collapse into the couch, limbs tangled around each other.

Five years old

With baby Adam in my arms, I step outside after dinner. Jack's been out with his dad all afternoon and he has a surprise he wants to show me. He picks up his bike and leads me to the alley.

"Ready?" his dad asks. Jack nods his head and kicks off from the pavement and zooms down the alley while Jay jogs beside him.

I balance the baby in my arm and hold up my phone to snap a photo. For the first time, Jack's riding his bike without training wheels! Jack turns around and beams at me.

"Wonderful, wonderful!" I cheer, smiling. My eyes smart with tears. What kind of adventures await my bike-riding boy? Who will he become?

I want to keep witnessing miracles woven into the fabric of our ordinary days. I want to be wowed over and over. But one day soon, both Adam and Jack will leave me behind and journey this world on their own. *God be with us,* I pray. Head held high, Jack races into the night.

"The days are long and the years are short," so goes the popular expression. Often we view time with a scarcity mindset—there's never enough—or lament that there's too much of it—I can't think of any more ways to entertain my children. All of Jack's movement milestones transpired on seemingly mundane days that likely included moments where I felt both pressed for time and wanting for more of it. Day in and day out, motherhood makes acutely aware of this tension. Anytime we witness a milestone is a chance to notice God's hands weaving grace into the fabric of ordinary time.

PRACTICE

Think about the last time you were surprised by your child's milestone. How did you mark it? What do you remember about how you felt? Thank God for the passing of time and the extraordinary moments in our ordinary days.

PRAYER

O God, my children have done it again
just yesterday they were dancing
and before that they were toddling

and now they're biking away from me
on their way to start their own journey
and though I'm overjoyed,
my heart's also breaking
each milestone a reminder
they don't belong to me, not really,
may I have faith enough to see these moments
as miracles—evidence of your abundant grace. Amen.

First Friendships
Sibling Love

Kim

We must always give thanks to God for you, brothers and sisters, as is right, because your faith is growing abundantly, and the love of every one of you for one another is increasing.

–2 Thessalonians 1:3

With sleepy eyes adjusting to the light, toddler Isaac stands in the corner of the crib reaching his arms to me and says, "I see Charlotte?" He's only been awake a few minutes, but wants to find his sister.

From first light, the two are drawn to one another.

Later in the day, while prepping dinner, I hear Isaac's cries from his crib, "Charlotte! Where are you? Charlotte, open my door!" Charlotte runs down the hall, the pitter-patter of her feet echoing, and opens Isaac's door.

"I'm here, Isaac!" Charlotte bellows while he bounces up and down in his crib.

"Read books?" she asks and plops herself on the bench next to him.

Throughout the day, the two are drawn to one another.

After watching episodes of PJ Masks and Spidey on Disney+ the kids don their face masks and capes and run through the house. "Superspeed, go!" Isaac stretches out his hands, a fist balled, and dashes down the hallway.

"We're superheroes to save the day!" They yell together in search of stuffed animals and dolls in need of rescuing. Where one goes, the other follows.

From year to year, the two are drawn to one another.

Picking up a few items at TJ Maxx, Isaac wanders the aisles and spots a pink and glittery water bottle with unicorns and ice cream cones. "Charlotte would love this water bottle," he tells me. "Can we get it for her?"

I watch from a distance—through the monitor, the rearview mirror, or while cooking dinner—and see the pull they have over each other, a deep

199

connection shared in laughter, bedtime hugs, dance parties, and spontaneous games of hide-and-seek. As sister and brother, these two have a rhythm of their own. An understanding that only they can decipher.

Children don't always get along. They have plenty of fights and sibling squabbles. Yet, when we witness the fullness of sibling relationships we catch a glimpse of God's persistent love for us. Whether your children can't seem to get along or are in a season where they are drawn to one another, the unfolding of our children's love mirrors the love that binds us all together in the body of Christ.

Charlotte loved Isaac before he was born, talking to him in the womb and kissing my belly. Her words, along with ours, were the most consistent voices he heard. Witnessing the affection my children have for one another inspires me—to see my neighbors as brothers and sisters and to love them as I have been loved. The gifts we pour into our children are not only meant for them, but to be shared. To be offered to the world drawing us closer to God and to one another.

TO PONDER

Think about your earliest relationships. Perhaps with your parents, siblings, or extended family and friends. What did you learn from them? How did they teach you to love and care for others?

PRAYER

Dear God, for the fullness of relationships, I thank you. We learn how to love and fight and forgive in our families. We learn to love unconditionally. We learn about you through the ways we connect and share and grow. Thank you for siblings and friends who become like family. Amen.

GRACE IN TRANSITIONS
NAVIGATING GROWING PAINS

Erin

I have loved you with an everlasting love;
therefore I have continued my faithfulness to you.

—Jeremiah 31:3

spent much of my twenties immersed in the world of triathlons. Triathlons
test endurance in three different sports: swimming, cycling, and running.
There are two points in every race when you need to switch from one sport
to the other: swimming to biking, and biking to running. When I was new
to triathlon, this mystified me. How did the elite triathletes transition so
gracefully?

That summer, I joined a triathlon training group that met near the shores
of Lake Michigan in Chicago. I can still picture the shimmering waves of the
lake and the city skyline rising up in view while I logged miles on the Lakefront
path. I'll never forget the icy rush of lake water whenever I had swim training.
Sessions included time with veteran athletes who coached us in each leg of the
sport, including the art of transitions.

The second transition in triathlon is extremely uncomfortable. Once you
park your bike, switch your shoes, and attempt to start running, you'll hit what
many endurance athletes call a wall. The lactic acid build up from cycling
makes your quadriceps feel like Jell-O, and you may feel like you'd rather stop
running and lie down on the hard pavement. For the less practiced athlete, the
shift can be jarring. Veteran athletes know you can't avoid it: no matter how
many times you move from bike to run, in between your legs will burn.

Motherhood is also marked by transitions. Children are constantly growing, and while we often pay most attention to their milestones, the space
between them—the transitions—can surprise us with their discomfort. When
our kids are learning to walk, we struggle with when to intervene and when

to let them tumble. When they're trying to make friends, we feel pain when they're excluded by peers and pray for the day they find their people.

The recent transition in our household is sending my oldest from preschool to kindergarten, while my youngest is moving from tummy time to full-out crawling. Our routines are changing quickly, and it's all a bit disorienting. I worry for my oldest as he leaves the comfort of his old preschool friends and starts over socially. I worry how to keep my youngest safe in a house filled with big boy toys that I'm constantly moving out of reach. As I navigate my children's differing needs—from homework help to narrating playtime—my attention stretches thin, and I worry I'm not enough for them.

I want to skip over the inherent challenge of parenting transitions. If it were my way, I'd prefer we hit each milestone, smooth and easy. Or maybe even hang back and relax in a familiar stage until I'm ready for change. Yet time keeps racing forward and so do my children.

Then I remember what it was like when my oldest dropped naps altogether at three. And when my youngest began eating solids. No matter how many times I experience a transition, I'm finding that a little pain is a part of the journey.

Some wisdom from the triathlon: You get a little more comfortable with the discomfort. You accept it, you stay humble. You jog through it, and with a little time, the burning sensation dissolves and you find your cadence.

Whether you're encountering a sleep regression, preparing for a big move, or struggling your way through your child's newfound independence, know you aren't alone in your children's transitions. Caught up in the pain of transition, I tend to forget about God's grace. But like the cheering squad on the sidelines of a race who calls your name and maybe even hands you a water bottle, God's grace can be found if you lift your eyes and look.

Watch for the people God's put in your journey, encouraging you from the sidelines. Your transitions might be painful, but the One who doesn't shy away from our pain or hard times will be there to comfort you. God's love for us is a constant we can count on amid the discomfort.

When your legs feel like Jell-O, grace will be there. When you break through the wall, grace will be there. Grace will be there, too, when you find your cadence as a mother.

TO PONDER

How do you respond to growing pains? Trust that God hasn't left your side. God cheers for you, even in these uncomfortable moments.

PRAYER

O God, once again, a new leg of this race has me shaken. Help me hear your voice cheering for me, encouraging me to keep moving. When change in my children stuns me, your love is a constant I can lean on for support. Amen.

FIGHTS WORTH FIGHTING
LEARNING TO COEXIST
WITH OTHERS

Kim

The commandment we have from him is this: those who love God
must love their brothers and sisters also.

–1 John 4:21

n the kitchen prepping dinner, Charlotte and Isaac's laughter float towards
me. "Look at this, Charlotte," Isaac says, "the tower is so high." "Let me put
another block on top," Charlotte adds, grabbing a rectangular block.

"Yes, let's see how high it will go!"

Blocks tumble and cheers erupt from both kids. I continue to hear the
knock of blocks as they get put back together. The kids are playing nicely. I
turn on a podcast while I chop and sauté, grateful for the time to myself in the
kitchen without distractions. Grateful that the kids are getting along.

But then Isaac yells, "That's mine, Charlotte. Give it back."

I keep chopping and wait for more pleading, and the eventual screams
when they both want the same toy.

This is what kids do: they go from being so kind and loving to one
another, to hitting and yelling and not being able to stand being in the same
room. Yet, they can't regulate themselves enough to know they need to step
away from each other. They haven't figured out how to give each other space.
So the fighting and yelling and tears continue, and my hands chop faster trying
to ignore the screams.

I've noticed that since my kids feel so safe with one another, nothing gets
held back. Yells, hits, red-faced tears, and stomping feet, it's all on the table.
Watching my kids fight, listening to them, and seeing their pain and frustration is hard to bear—I want to step in and referee. I desire kindness and sharing.

Yet, this fighting is part and parcel of sibling relationships. I believe that
the fights my children have with one another provide a learning ground for

fights and challenges that they will face in their lives. The way they engage with each other is practice for how they can interact with others as they get older. I hope as they grow they learn to fight with conviction, to speak up, and to use their voice to bring forth a more just and peaceful world. I also expect that they will listen to others, learning and growing from a multitude of different perspectives.

The everyday sibling squabbles over who gets to sit next to mom, who pours the flour into the mixing bowl, and who can play with the racetrack prepare them to learn what's fair and not, to learn when to stand up and help others, and when to allow others to handle their own battles. In day-to-day fights, kids learn when to hold a boundary and when to let someone else have their own way. In our families we practice relationship-building, the give and take, offering and asking for forgiveness, and then we take all we've learned into our communities. Whether a church community or a playgroup or neighborhood, we're all faced with how to interact with others. We have to make decisions on when to speak up and when to let others figure out for themselves the way forward.

The Bible tells us: love God and love others (Matthew 22: 37-39). The call to love is not easy, and we know this truth. Yet, we also know the truth of God's love binding us together to one another and walking with us in the challenges of relationships. Whenever we fight, we trust God is near, forever encouraging us to follow the way of Jesus.

TO PONDER

Do you have sibling relationships or other friendships that are fraught with fighting? Pray for guidance on how God is working in your heart to transform the relationship. Reflect on what you can learn from the challenges you face with others and how you can take those lessons into other experiences.

PRAYER

Dear God, give me patience when my children are fighting. Help me to know when to step in and when to let them fight their own battles. Give me peace when they are hurting. Give me strength to lead with compassion. And together, may we all work towards fighting for the good of all. Amen.

WELCOMING A LITTLE ONE
EXPANDING YOUR FAMILY

Erin

Whoever welcomes one such child in my name welcomes me.

–Mark 9:37

reparing for our second son brought several conversations. When we met with our pediatrician, he spoke with five-year-old Jack about welcoming his little brother. "There's going to be a little crying," he warned, referring to the new baby.

In the hospital after Adam was born, we video called my in-laws, who were watching Jack, and introduced them all to Adam. "Jack-Jack," I said, holding his swaddled brother toward the phone camera, "This is your new baby brother, Adam."

At the sound of his brother's name, Jack began wailing. "I wanted to name the baby," he gulped, scrunching up his face.

"Oh honey…" I said, glancing up at my husband. "I'm sorry about that, but Daddy and I decided on Adam." Jack's tears weren't the ones his pediatrician had alluded to, but I knew this wouldn't be the last time Jack (or any of us) would shed tears about this transition.

By the time Jay and I brought Adam home, Jack warmed to his brother. He peered over the baby car seat, a smile splaying over his lips. "Hel-lo, Ad-am!" he said, lifting his intonation. Watching him gaze at his brother made me smile, too. Our family had grown to include another sweet boy, and I was eager to watch their relationship develop.

As the months drew on, Jack grew more comfortable with his little brother's presence. He made up songs for his brother and learned to kiss him on the head at bedtime. He came up with nicknames for him—"Adam Smash" and "delicate diamond." At school, Jack proudly shared with his classmates that he'd become a brother.

While Adam grew and changed from a snoozy peanut to an alert and active rug rat, I delighted in his response to his big brother's welcome. His eyes lit up at the sight of Jack, taking in each move he made. Sometimes, Adam's little fingers would rake and claw to find Jack's head if he was nearby his brother. When they played on the floor, Adam liked to gnaw on Jack's knee or hand to relieve teething pressure.

Both boys' tears continued, of course, and frustrations that accompany any major shift in family dynamics. One day I was writing in my journal and a melancholy I couldn't shake overtook me. Setting down my pen, I realized I'd been so consumed with caring for Adam, I hadn't spent much time with Jack, who was being tended to by his father. I missed my first baby.

Welcoming another baby into a family is a significant change for parents and their children. We worry how we'll divide our time between multiple kids and all the chores in our household. Our older kids may pine for our attention even more than before, perhaps displaying some developmental regressions. We wonder how to convey to them that, just because a new baby's arrived, our love for them hasn't wavered.

From that point forward, I decided to become more intentional with cultivating one-to-one time with Jack. While the baby napped, we'd bake muffins. After an early bedtime for the baby, I'd sit with him while he watched Ninjago on Netflix. Sometimes we played soccer in the yard or we'd snuggle up and read library books together.

Once, Jack noticed his brother crying while I was out of the nursery and ran to find me. "Mommy," he exhaled. "You need to teach 'Swing Low' to Adam!" Together we stood at the crib and hummed the lullaby, a favorite of Jack's, while I rocked Adam and laid him down to rest.

It is a privilege to raise children, and to welcome them as Jesus does. Jesus knew that welcoming children meant experiencing crying, tantrums, sibling squabbles, and growing pains. Yet Jesus continually calls the little children to him, inviting us to do the same, knowing that our hearts don't break when we welcome more children, they just expand.

PRACTICE

Welcoming a new child into your home breaks and rebuilds existing family dynamics, transforming our roles and faith. In what ways did your family evolve to welcome a new baby? How have you seen love manifest—in other siblings, in spouses, in yourself? How do you cultivate relationships with your individual children? Find a moment to thank God for the opportunity to raise them. Name what you love about each child, including the spiritual gifts you've observed. Take time to share these words of praise with your kids, too.

PRAYER

Dear God, you know well the joy and upheaval that comes with welcoming a child. Thank you for blessing me with little ones to nurture. Foster compassion, grace, and love in my ever-changing family. Guide me as I aim to love each child in my care with tenderness and special attention. May I model welcome to all of God's children, trusting in the promise of your perfect son whose love transforms us all. In your name I pray. Amen.

"ARE WE THERE YET?"

BEING PRESENT

Kim

Finally, beloved, whatever is true, whatever is honorable, whatever
is just, whatever is pure, whatever is pleasing, whatever is
commendable, if there is any excellence and if there is anything
worthy of praise, think about these things.

—Philippians 4:8

O n a recent vacation we heard the common phrase from our kids,
"Are we there yet?" Their understanding of time couldn't comprehend the amount of hours it'd take to reach our destination. Yet,
too often, I'm not that different from my children. I find myself asking my
own version of "are we there yet?" Whether it's with my writing, parenting, or
planning the next adventure, I'm always waiting for what's next. I look ahead
to the upcoming nap or quiet time, phone call, school year, vacation, meal, or
educational opportunity and wonder, "Am I there yet?" It seems that I'm always
waiting for what's next, rather than living in the here and now.

Motherhood demands so much of us—physically, mentally, and emotion-
ally. We're tired and worn down from lack of sleep. Our minds race with to-do's
and checklists and all the appointments to schedule. Words and images and
other people bombard us with the best way to raise children and the most
helpful products, or simply tell us we're doing it wrong. We are never lacking
for information and support. Too often it can feel like we're racing through
our days and anticipating what is to come. Chatting with other mothers, we
compare sleep schedules and what our kids eat, sometimes lamenting that ours
aren't quite feeding themselves yet or able to self-soothe. We can find ourselves
longing for the next season.

We dream about the day all our children will be in full-time school or
reading on their own. Our calendars fill with camps, playdates, vacations, and
experiences to anticipate, sometimes forgetting to remember to practice the

presence of now. We want to check off the milestones of eating solids, crawl-ing, walking, and sleeping through the night rather than dwell in the season we're living. Perhaps that's because a season with young children is especially demanding—but it brings its own gifts, too.

In the car on the way to vacation when the kids asked, "Are we there yet?", I'd answer: "No, we're not there yet, but why don't you tell me what you see right here." The kids turned their heads to gaze out the window and began rattling off what they saw:

Trees, birds, a red car, the sun reflecting on the road, yellow wildflowers, cows, mommy and daddy…

I nodded in agreement with the kids as their voices raised with the new things they saw. For a few moments, we all marveled at the sights before us. The landscape changed from hills to flatland and we could see for miles. I thought to myself, we're not there yet, but we're here. And right here is enough; this moment is a gift.

Are you asking yourself or your family, "Are we there yet?" It's natural to look ahead and dream about the future, but it's also important to be where we are now. Wherever you are, look and listen. Whatever is before you, what do you see? How does the light fall in your home? What sounds do you hear from your yard and neighborhood? Look at your lives and see the miracles and mys-teries before you. Stop and see your children and yourself as you are in this very moment—alive, loved, and God's beloved.

PRACTICE

Take time to be where you are with full attention. Bring a notebook and pen and make a list of what you see and hear. Offer a prayer for God to meet you right now.

PRAYER

God, help me to be still and present. Teach me to live my life in this moment, the one right now; the minutes and hours that you're giving to me this day. Sometimes I see whatever is hard or difficult in front of me, but I want to be drawn to whatever is good. Whenever I smell breast milk on my shirt and break up another sibling fight, help me to be here now. Whenever I can't make it to drink a hot cup of coffee and forget to eat my own lunch, help me to stay present to the people and tasks before me. Give me grace to see these days as gifts and this life full of your beauty. Amen.

BIRTHDAY BLESSINGS
MARKING MILESTONES

Erin

I came that they may have life, and have it abundantly.

—John 10:10

On a muggy day in July, we gathered at a local splash pad with 20 preschoolers and their parents to celebrate my son Jack's 5 ½ birthday. Earlier this year, on his true birthday, Jack told me he wanted a party with all his friends, but I declined. It was winter, and I had two days until my scheduled C-section. Instead, I promised Jack we'd do something fun in the summer, after the baby came, for his half birthday.

After booking the venue, sending the invites, and ordering the food, I watched as Jack's long-promised party unfolded. Children arrived in bright swimsuits bearing gift bags bulging with tissue paper. My son ran laps around the premises greeting his friends with glee. I welcomed guests and corralled the crowd toward the pizza and cupcakes. The kids laughed and soaked themselves on a pirate-themed splash pad. The vibe of the day was liquid joy.

Once the gifts were put away and the trash was collected, I realized something. I'd been so busy hosting, I had no photos to show for it. We didn't take enough pictures.

To some, such a party might seem frivolous, and thus, the need for photos is as well. Yet, after two years of avoiding big gatherings out of a concern for contagion, this event was an opening, a carpe diem moment, a means of reclaiming our social life after months of shifting plans due to an ever-evolving virus. Our family needed this celebration.

Birthdays are milestones during which we can honor our children's coming of age and our labors accompanying their growth. They're a time to thank God for the beauty of our children and acknowledge the way they shape our souls. On birthdays we take photos, shower our kids with extra attention and presents, share our favorite stories. Mostly, they're cause for feasting and fun.

God made us to be in community with each other, and I believe that God revels in our felicity.

Lift up birthdays but also little moments with your children—a big win, a special concert, when they finally learn to read. The way you mark them doesn't have to look fancy, just special to your family. Take every opportunity to relish the miracle of their lives and give thanks to our Creator who fashioned them out of love.

This is what I want to remember from my son's half birthday: Him racing bare-chested in the grass with the neighbor kiddos. A cooler full of Capri Suns. Lou Malnati's cheese pizza. Two kinds of cupcakes: chocolate and vanilla. Conversation and smiles and way too many boxes of Legos. Preschoolers rushing down a water slide belly first and giggling.

We didn't take enough pictures, but I have a clear picture in my memory: a smiling boy surrounded in love. That will be enough.

PRACTICE

Write a letter or prayer for your child on their birthday, reflecting on the Spirit's movement in their life. Save the note in an email or special folder set aside for them to keep when they're older.

PRAYER

Inhale: God, in our feasting you are with us.
Exhale: You are worthy of praise.

Opting Out (For Now)
Seasons of Rest

Kim

For everything there is a season, and a time for every matter under heaven.

–Ecclesiastes 3:1

id-Facebook scroll I stop and pause. Before me I see a handful of young girls, arms draped over each other's shoulders, helmets atop their head, and smiles across their faces. I recognize a few of the girls from Charlotte's class. The caption reads: *What a great season of softball, so much growth and learning for all these girls! Good job, ladies!* Clicking to the page, I start at the top and work my way down seeing more and more teams posing for pictures. The end of the baseball and softball season stats and congratulations fills the gaps in between photos. Beneath each photo parents and friends comment: *Thank you coaches! We can't wait to see what's in store for this group in the years ahead!* With each picture and each comment, my own internal dialogue picks up: Charlotte's not pictured because she didn't play. She's missed out on learning a skill. She's not getting the same experience in a team sport. Her friends are getting closer without her.

Picture after picture I wonder if we made the wrong decision. Saying no can be hard, even with good reason.

My husband and I intentionally decided to have Charlotte do one more year of T-ball rather than traveling softball. The time commitment was shorter, and all the practices and games were in our town. We opted for ease. Yet, I couldn't help but feel like she was missing out when I saw all the team pictures.

But when I would look at Charlotte, I recognized my own insecurities were at play.

For the month of T-ball, Charlotte delighted in hitting the ball and running the bases. She waved to her friends on both teams. She slung the bat over her shoulder, glove in hand, and skipped to the fields. For her, she was right where she wanted to be. It's me, her mom, who needs to remember her growth is not a race. There's no competition for how many activities I have my children participate in. But it's easier said than done, and when I see other children my kids' age with skills and team building experience, I feel a longing. I feel like we're missing out. Yet, Charlotte is involved. She's engaged with friends. She has experiences that are forming her. And most importantly, these activities are on our timeline. They work for our family right now. I'm the one who needs the reminder to not feel guilty that our schedules don't look the same as others.

Charlotte missing one season of softball is just that—a season. Seasons come and go. That's the gift of them—we experience them and get to move on to something new. There's learning in each of them and in the transitions. There's learning in saying no, too, and in providing space for what could be. There will always be something to do and somewhere to go and something to sign up for, a new experience, a sport, an extracurricular. Our kids will not experience a lack. But for right now, I want to lean into the moments where we choose to say no and to see what emerges in saying yes to more space, more time, and more family. Saying no has allowed room to marvel at God's creation and the laughter of my children; moments sitting across the table with my family talking and playing games; offering prayers for God's people.

Whatever season you're experiencing, whether driving to and from practices and rehearsals and games, or savoring the time with no commitments, trust that you're right where you are meant to be. In the passing of time and the learning, in the saying yes and saying no, God meets you as seasons come and go.

TO PONDER

What are you saying *no* to in this season? Make a list and then reflect on how God is inviting you to say *yes* to something else.

PRAYER

God, I'm trying not to compare. I'm trying to focus on what's best for my family. But there's so much vying for my attention, and so many opportunities we could take. Help me to see the gift of saying *no*. Help me to say *yes* to rest, laughter around the table, slow mornings, and moments to look deep in my family's eyes. Give me peace in knowing that seasons come and go. More of you, and less worry. Amen.

THE GIFTS
OF OTHER MOTHERS
FRIENDSHIP

Erin

> Therefore encourage one another and build up each other, as indeed you are doing.
>
> —1 Thessalonians 5:11

After I left my job to stay home with my children, I knew I needed a wider circle of support. As connections with work colleagues I'd known for nearly a decade faded, isolation ate away at me. Many of the stay-at-home moms in my neighborhood shared childcare, meals, and their lives with each other. I longed for that kind of friendship, but I wasn't sure how to find it. With an infant and preschooler in my care, I often felt stuck at home due to the baby's sleep and feeding schedule.

That spring, I watched the rain bead against the windows while I was relegated to the rocking chair, nursing Adam. Hours and days dripped by, punctuated by Jack's preschool pickup and my husband's return from the office. This new stage of motherhood surprised me with its loneliness.

While wiping counters and putting away clean onesies, I started praying for a few good mom friends: *God, help me find some mom friends—friends to text for parenting advice, friends whose children will love mine, friends to call on when we need a helping hand, friends to sweeten our days.*

When school let out for the summer, our neighborhood teemed with children. Chalk marked the sidewalk and children's laughter drifted in the breeze. Adam's schedule grew less demanding, so I started taking my boys with me to the playground whenever we had a break.

There I met Lyndsay, mom to a six-year-old boy and a baby girl a few months older than Adam. Like me, she'd stepped back from work after having her second child. She had an ease and warmth about her that was undeniably special. We held our babes and watched our boys chase each other around the playground. We talked about milestones and sleep woes, family and work. We exchanged numbers and planned the first of many playdates for our children. I didn't know it at the time, but she was an answer to my prayers.

She wasn't the only answer, either. While Jack was at summer camp, I took Adam on stroller walks and met up with Jill and Brigit, moms I knew from my neighborhood book club. Like me, they loved to read and write. We shared advice and stories in person and on a text thread. We carried on conversations while pushing swings and strollers. We sipped coffee and laughed and cried and wrangled our kids together.

As summer went on, I connected with moms at my son's preschool for playdates and other neighbor moms with kids close in age to Jack and Adam. Each of these women was kind and generous to our family, making efforts to welcome and include my boys in her children's circle.

Connections budded and blossomed. Summer days flowed by quickly, brightened by playdates and conversation. By the time school was about to start, I had a new prayer to say throughout my daily chores: *Thank you God for filling my life with wonderful women—moms I looked up to, laughed with and cared for—a new village of encouragement and grace.*

God made us to be in relationship with one another, and motherhood is sweetened by the companionship of other mothers. We all need someone to marvel with us at life's rainbows and someone to hold an umbrella for us in life's storms. We all need a knowing glance, a word of wisdom, someone to help us cheer on our children. What's more, our kids need to see us making friends and modeling healthy relationships. We need the gifts of other mothers.

Sometimes it feels like all the other moms know each other on the playground. Or you just aren't in the clique. Don't give up. Trust that there are mamas out there just like you, praying for friendship. Keep yourself open to new possibilities, friendships springing up in the middle of the neighborhood, school functions, soccer sidelines.

Pay attention to the moms around you who build you up and build up your children. Listen to their stories and tell them yours. Make them meals, make playdates with their kids, make new stories together. When you reach milestones, celebrate together. When you experience your inevitable low points, lean on your friends who will carry you forward when you can walk no further. Soon you'll look around and discover you've built a beautiful circle of support.

TO PONDER

Who has shown you support in your mothering journey? What relationships with other mothers do you want to deepen? Give thanks to God for the gifts of other mothers, and ask God to help you show support to the mothers in your circle.

PRAYER

Dear God,
you made your people to be in relationship with one another.
Embolden me to answer your call
to go out into the world and love my neighbors.
Lead me to other mothers—
to nurturing friendships—
women I can accompany
on this mothering journey.
In your name I pray.
Amen.

THE WOMEN AT THE WELL
SEASONS OF NURTURING COMMUNITY

Kim

The woman said to him, "Sir, give me this water, so that I may never
be thirsty or have to keep coming here to draw water."

–John 4: 15

Before marriage and kids, before seminary and serving as a pastor, I
lived in The Gambia, West Africa as a Peace Corps volunteer. Every
day I spent time with the women. Situated in the center of the village,
women walked to the pump to fill their buckets in the early morning. Women
gathered at the well, sharing joys and challenges, news of babies and marriages,
the tediousness of preparing food. I joined in on the laughter and jokes, and
got to know the women.

At the well, I learned the power in being present to stories and the power
of listening to ease burdens. I saw women help carry a friend's bucket of water
to bring relief, and witnessed all the women caring and mothering the children.
Women came with babies on their backs, older girls joined in the pumping of
the water, and all ages stood together and told stories. Together, we shared in
the collective task of showing up to one another.

As a young woman at this time, I received the gifts given to me freely from
the women at the well. It wasn't just how to carry a bucket more easily or how
to use the water more efficiently. They shared stories about their history and
culture. They helped me feel less alone.

In motherhood, we all want to receive this living water from God, and we
also want to be a bearer of the living water to others. We can all be bearers of
grace wherever mothers gather: weekly playdates, the grocery line wrangling
food and children, and church pews. We can offer a hand, listen with attention, bear the burdens of other mothers, and walk side by side. These actions
can help lighten the weight of worry, fear, and questioning. An encouraging
text during a family transition, dropping food on the porch during a busy

week, holding a mama's hand as they face a diagnosis—all living water. When another mother wonders whether she's doing enough and if she *is* enough, we can be there to offer a resounding *yes*.

This living water offered to me from others pours into all aspects of my life, drenching me in God's grace and love. When the thoughts come unwanted into my mind of not doing enough, when I'm yelling at my kids, when there's another snack request, I need to know that Jesus meets me at the well to fill me up. Desiring his presence, I turn to him with open hands. "Give me this water, Jesus."

This is your story, too. Jesus meets you and loves you and is never afraid to be with you in the hard places of your life. Nothing is too dark for Jesus. Nothing is too hard for Jesus. Jesus calls to you: *Come and drink, come and be filled with my love.*

Because Jesus pours his grace into us every hour of every day, we get to offer this same life-giving water to other mothers. We can be their well, their safe place, their comfort, their listening ear, their words of encouragement when the waters are dry: *you're doing great, mama, you're the precise right mother for your kids, keep going.*

TO PONDER

Picture yourself at the well with Jesus. Tell him what's on your heart. Where do you need to be filled up with this living water? Imagine Jesus with you offering his presence and love.

PRAYER

God of Living Water, your love quenches my thirst, it satisfies me when I'm feeling lost and lonely, it renews me when I'm tired. Yet, sometimes I need the reminder that this water is for me. On days when I'm searching for you, cover me in your grace. In the moments when I'm questioning my worth, pour out your mercy. Keep your love raining down on me, so that I can share this goodness with others. Amen.

Ultimate Superhero
Grace Over Perfection
in Motherhood

Erin

The LORD is my shepherd, I shall not want.
He makes me lie down in green pastures;
he leads me beside still waters;
he restores my soul.

–Psalm 23:1-3

Donning a royal blue mask and superhero cape, Jack zooms from the playroom into the kitchen. "If you're in danger, give me a call!" he shouts, whizzing past me on the way to his bedroom.

Watching my son play superheroes delights me and makes me long for the simplicity of my childhood. Pausing in front of a mound of dirty dishes, I wish a superhero could swoop in and save me from this mess. Come to think of it, I could use a superhero to save me from the laundry mountain in Jack's bedroom and the bathroom that needs cleaning.

I turn on the faucet, grab the dish brush and begin rinsing. I remember my mother as Wonder Woman. During my school years, she worked full-time as a teacher and our church's music director. On top of that, she raised my brother and me, handled meals, chores, lesson plans and more with apparent ease. She always showed up early to work and fulfilled her duties with a smile, and she's always been my biggest fan. Now that I'm a mom myself, I imagine my mom experienced the same tension I struggle with in keeping up with my kids and work and household, but I never noticed it as a child.

Setting the dishes on the rack, I think, I want to be Wonder Woman, too. I want to make the perfect school lunch that actually gets eaten, follow the right parenting methodology for my kids, limit screentime, connect them with good friends who are kind, volunteer at school, and protect them from

221

the world's many dangers. Caught up in my quest for perfection, I overextend myself and bring myself to the brink of exhaustion.

"If you're in danger, give me a call!" Jack says, brushing past me again. Something I often forget: I can call the ultimate superhero when I'm in the midst of worry and stress over parenting. Psalm 23 teaches that God shepherds and restores our souls, even when we are at our lowest. Even when we lose our way, the Shepherd pursues us. God will never abandon us. God is our ultimate superhero.

The psalmist declares "I shall not want": these words comfort me when I feel anxious or afraid in my faith journey. If I examine my heart, sometimes I strive and push in my mothering because I want so much to be blameless. I want people to like me. I want my kids to like me. I twist the gospel and act as if I need to earn God's favor. Psalm 23 says I don't have to be Wonder Woman—I can put down the cape, stop pretending and allow myself to be vulnerable with God. I don't need to be "perfect" to receive God's grace.

When you struggle with your shortcomings as a mom, or worry about past missteps with your kids, God declares to you: you are enough. There is no wanting or lacking in the eyes of God. God loves you and made you on purpose to answer this call to love your children. Turn to the One whose perfect love restores and rescues us.

PRACTICE

The next time you feel overwhelmed in your mothering journey, pause what you're doing and recite your favorite line from Psalm 23, such as "The Lord is my shepherd."

PRAYER

Shepherding God,
guide my posture
from striving to surrender
pride to humility
controlling to trusting your work
as the Ultimate Superhero
my source of perfect grace.
Amen.

IMAGINE
THE BEAUTY OF MOTHERHOOD

Kim

I will give thanks to the LORD with my whole heart; I will tell of all your wonderful deeds. I will be glad and exult in you; I will sing praise to your name, O Most High.

–Psalm 9:1-2

At the dining room table, surrounded by fixings for tacos, Charlotte stands and turns to Isaac. "Imagine the whole school was made of donuts!" Isaac tips his head back in laughter. "Oh my goodness, that would be amazing. We'd have to eat them to get everywhere!"

"Imagine the whole school was made of desks," he adds and both kids erupt in laughter.

"Imagine the school was a pool!"

Between bites of dinner and bouncing on their seats, the kids go back and forth adding more and more details and hilarious scenes. This imagining must have originated at school, or maybe a TV show. I'm not sure, but since that first dinner conversation, both kids delight in imagining together. Throughout the day the kids will say "Imagine," and launch into a series of funny scenarios, becoming more and more ridiculous as they go. Together they laugh at each other's descriptions.

Sometimes I'll steer them back to seriousness, "Imagine you finished eating your dinner," or "Imagine we didn't take each other's toys and yell at each other." But most times I laugh along and wonder with them.

Their questions prompt me to ask myself: What do I imagine?

I imagine a world where I don't need to fear for my kids' safety in school.

I imagine growing old with my husband and celebrating birthdays and holidays together.

I imagine traveling across the world.

I imagine a garden full of produce and cabinets loaded with canned fruits and veggies.

I imagine deepening friendships.

I imagine peace.

I imagine communities caring for all.

I imagine conversations and deep listening across differences.

I imagine hope, love, and mercy.

I also imagine a clean house with no toys to trip over, dishes put away, meals already prepared and cooked for me. I imagine not having to fret about my kids making friends. I imagine restful nights and no more Google searches on symptoms and learning disorders. I imagine never losing my temper.

But then I look at my life, these children, this home we're creating and inhabiting, these other mothers and friends, and I don't have to imagine. Because this life, now, is full of beauty and hope; this is what I've been gifted, and this life is all mine to steward.

You have your own imaginings and dreams of the heart—we all do. God knows what you dream, and is with you to see the life before you as holy. The Lord of all invites you to dream big—for yourself, your kids, and the world—but I believe God also calls us to witness the miracles that are already in our lives.

God's presence fills every nook and cranny of our lives; God's grace pulls up a seat at the dinner table; God's mercy holds us when we sleep and when we wake. We fall on our knees in gratitude: holding small hands, kissing squishy cheeks, saying prayers together, cradling a sleeping baby, offering and asking for forgiveness, cuddling with movies and popcorn on the couch, walking to school, and playing at the park.

Imagine, God whispers in your ear, *this is your life. Do you see it? Do you feel it? Take a look around, and see the beauty of motherhood.*

PRACTICE

What do you imagine? Make a list. Make another list of what you're thankful for today. Give thanks for the dreams and imaginings of your heart that have already been gifted to you.

PRAYER

God of all, thank you for this life. I'm in awe of the beauty of motherhood. May I continue to look at my life and see your fingerprints all around me. From first watch to falling asleep in bed, turn me to gratitude. From sticky hands to bubble-filled baths, draw me into your love. From the first whispers of hope for a baby to celebrating birthdays, cover me in grace. For these children and for families and friends, thank you. Beauty surrounds me. Thanks be to God. Amen.

Beauty on the Path
Seeing Ourselves
Through God's Eyes

Erin

As a mother comforts her child,
so I will comfort you;
you shall be comforted in Jerusalem.

—Isaiah 66:13

Adam refused to sleep in his crib. An ill-timed car nap had disrupted my youngest's afternoon nap, and I needed a way to get him some rest. We'd been struggling with sleep: one day, my four-month-old would sleep well, and the next, he'd be up and down all night. I walked up and down the halls with Adam in my arms, gazing out the window. Summer sunlight beckoned me outdoors.

Craving respite, I packed Adam in the stroller, laced up my walking shoes and headed out the door, toward the neighboring walking path. Within a couple minutes, he fell asleep in the stroller, and I found myself alone with my thoughts.

Adam was my second child, but mothering him was challenging me in new ways. I kept thinking another mom might have his sleep mastered by now. Nursing him consumed my time and I often fell into bed exhausted at the end of a long day, only to be woken up a couple hours later. I couldn't remember the last time I'd showered, but no matter, I was outside, and the sun was warming my shoulders and Adam was still sleeping. I checked under the lid of the baby stroller and watched his chest rise and fall, then adjusted the blanket to cover his legs from direct sunlight.

A crop of buttercup flowers burst into view. White butterflies twirled among them, and I smiled at my luck catching them here. No matter how many times I had walked this path, something beautiful always surprised me.

My grin dropped when I noticed a gaggle of guys crowding at the edge of the bridge ahead of me. They had to be in their late teens or early twenties, and instantly they made me feel self-conscious. I longed for my pre-baby self, the one who moved swiftly down the lakeshore path in coordinated jogging wear, checking her watch to see if she'd made her nine-minute mile pace. Today I hunched over the stroller, hair piled on a bird's nest bun, wearing ratty leggings and an old top smelling of spit up.

When I approached their spot and stopped to see what they were looking at, they barely noticed me. I flipped on the stroller breaks and followed their gaze. Across the river stood a doe and her fawn with tan-colored short hair and white markings. The doe nuzzled her youngest, who was drinking from the river. She looked up now and then, but otherwise watched her fawn. I stayed there, breathless with wonder, until Adam rustled in his stroller. I couldn't help but think God put this deer in my path for a reason.

It was a mother that stopped us in our tracks with her beauty.

It was a mother.

Maybe today you are reading this devotion and feeling less than beautiful. Perhaps, like me, you're feeling a little worn down and in need of some TLC. Maybe you're struggling with a child's diagnosis or with marital discord, or longing for a younger version of yourself. You might be staring down negative pregnancy tests or waiting for answers. You could be facing a difficult parenting stage or struggling with your children's growing independence. However this devotion meets you, I hope you take a step back and see yourself with God's adoring eyes.

This doe is beautiful for the way she mothers.

And so are you.

PRACTICE

Put yourself in the path of beauty. You don't have to go far to do it, simply shift your awareness. Step in front of the mirror or into your home. Try visiting a place you've never been, such as an art museum, or a place you frequent, such as a walking path. Make a list of the beautiful things you love, then thank God for those blessings.

PRAYER

Gracious God,
turn my eyes to meet yours,
help me see myself as you do:

Like a doe bending in the wild
to nourish her growing fawn,
I am beloved and beautiful.

Turn my gaze to those around me,
so I might reflect your love
to them, too. Amen.

Afterword

You, dear mama, have been in our prayers. It's been our dream to walk alongside you and share stories of God's grace breaking through in our motherhood journeys. We pray you found comfort and refreshment in the pages of this devotional, and we hope our words shed light on the holiness all around us.

We wrote these devotions in the fringe hours of our days—early mornings and after bedtime, during naptime and while nursing a baby, in the carpool line and at the doctor's office—and while we wrote, we imagined you reading our words in similar times and spaces. Thank you for letting us accompany you throughout your days.

Each of these devotions are words we still need to hear, Good News we need to be reminded of—daily. These are stories we hope made you feel less alone in this sacred calling. At the same time, we know our stories only show a fraction of the diverse expressions of motherhood, and we pray these words will encourage you to claim your stories in community with other mothers. For we know that we mother and live and love best in community. We listen to one another. We learn from one another. We share. We grow.

Now it's your turn. Your motherhood story is important and is ready to be heard. Pick up a pen, your phone, or a camera. Claim the beauty of your days, notice where God is moving, and invite others into your world.

The beauty of motherhood is yours
in this moment and stage,
in your worry, pride, love, and rage,
in cutting veggies and grapes,
in kissing cuts and scrapes,
in building Legos and blocks,
in playing with bubbles and chalk,

in rocking children to sleep,
in all the memories you keep.

Let these words remind you
as you grapple in faith
you're never alone,
you're drenched in God's grace.

The call to mother—
a challenge and a treasure
bestowing you with the name forever:
Mama.

Acknowledgements

im: As a family we've found that offering prayers of thanks throughout the day keeps us oriented to God's goodness in our midst. Whether we're in the car driving to school, around the table for a meal, or walking around town we find pockets of time to lift up our thanks. Similarly, throughout the writing of this book, gratitude for so many people kept popping up.

Erin, I remember our first phone call where I pitched articles to *Living Lutheran*. I was sitting at the dining room table during naptime. Who knew from that first call we'd develop not only a working relationship but a deep friendship. Thank you for following the work of the Spirit and bringing this book and our dreams of being published authors to life. Here's to more hours of Voxer chats and Google docs.

Trinity McFadden and The Bindery, thank you for believing in this book from the first email and phone call. For all the ways you've been our cheerleader, thank you.

Church Publishing Incorporated, thank you for saying yes to our book. Eve Strillacci, you joined us in this process at just the right time. Thank you for the encouragement, your listening ear, and all the ways you made this book better.

So many creative mothers have poured into this project. To Fay, Melissa, Jessica, and Jenn, let's keep writing and sharing. To the ladies of Exhale, you inspire me daily with your persistence in doing the work and bearing witness to motherhood. To the C+C team, thank you for believing that motherhood and creativity can coexist and that we're all better for it when we tell our stories.

Sara, Erica, and Annika, thank you for the well-timed texts and notes of encouragement.

My playgroup friends, thank you for showing up every week and being our tribe.

Jenna Brack and Callie Feyen, you made these devotions sing. Your support and encouragement have been invaluable. Thank you for offering your gifts and kneeling beside us in prayer.

My mom, thanks for being my first reader and biggest cheerleader.

And finally, to Stephen, Charlotte, and Isaac, thank you for making this life beautiful. I love you.

rin: The Beauty of Motherhood came into being through countless Voxer messages, texts, emails, Google docs, and phone calls. In the spring of 2021, Kim and I were working on separate writing projects when, in a moment that can only be described as an act of the Spirit, the idea for this book imprinted itself on our hearts. Together, we crafted a proposal that propelled us onto the rollercoaster ride of authorship. As co-authors Kim and I are keenly aware that books are not born in isolation, and many thanks are due to all who labored with us to create this devotional.

Kim, writing alongside you over the years has been an absolute gift, and to publish a book together is even sweeter. What began as a professional connection has blossomed into a life-giving partnership and friendship. For that, I'm deeply grateful. Thank you for emboldening me to share my stories and faith, and for your willingness to go first.

To our agent, Trinity, and the good folks at The Bindery Agency, thank you for championing this book from first pitch to publication. It's a blessing to have you in our corner.

To Airié, Eve, and the entire team at Church Publishing Incorporated, thank you for believing in this book and bringing it into the world with us. We're so grateful to you for saying yes.

Jenna, thank you for the pep talks, prayers, and thoughtful feedback on initial drafts for this collection. Your help was a godsend.

Callie, a couple years ago you led me through a writing intensive that would be instrumental to my growth as a writer. I'm indebted to you for the wisdom you've shared about craft, faith, and catching light. Thank you for being this book's fairy godmother. You made our stories sparkle.

Gratitude to the women of our writing group—Fay, Jenn, Jess, and Melissa—for their endless support, including reading drafts, cheering us on, and prayers. Thanks to writer-mamas Amanda, Kelsi, Julia, Lindsay, and Ojus for their support and friendship. I'm grateful to Ashlee and the entire Exhale Creativity community for fostering a safe space to share our art and our lives. You mamas are a breath of fresh air, and you inspire and encourage me daily.

To all the mom friends I know and love, especially my best friend Holly and my neighbors Lyndsay, Brigit, and Jill: Thank you for loving me and my children well, and for making the heavy work of motherhood feel lighter.

To my former colleagues at the ELCA churchwide organization, especially the *Living Lutheran* magazine team, thank you for your friendship and for all you taught me about faithful storytelling.

To the good people and pastors of my congregation—I'm deeply grateful to you for being my family's faith home for a decade. For your radical welcome, for creating space for doubt and exploration, for the peace and grace, for nurturing us and our kids in faith, thank you.

Thanks upon thanks are due to my amazing family for supporting my writing career, especially my dad, my brother and sister-in-law, my grandmothers, and my in-laws.

Mom, I truly think of you as Wonder Woman. Thanks for your encouragement and help at every step of this author journey, from reading my writings to providing childcare, coffee gift cards and prayers. I'm blessed to be mothered by you.

Jay, I'm always aware that it must be hard to be married to a writer, but you've only encouraged me to pursue my art. Thank you for taking care of me, and being on the same team as me. I know that I am the luckiest. I love you.

My beautiful children, Jack and Adam, thank you for waking me up to glimmers of grace hidden in the ordinary. It is the honor of my life to be your mother. Words cannot express how much I love you, but this book is my best attempt.

Finally, to you, dear reader: thank you for coming on this journey with us. It's been a dream come true to share these stories with you.

ABOUT THE AUTHORS

Kimberly Knowle-Zeller is a writer, pastor in the Evangelical Lutheran Church in America, and mother of two. She writes on the intersection of faith and parenting, searching for holiness in the ordinary. Her widely acclaimed stories on faith and motherhood have appeared in *The Christian Century*, *Living Lutheran*, *Episcopal Café*, *Coffee + Crumbs*, and more. She lives in Cole Camp, Missouri. Connect with her on Instagram (@kknowlezeller) and at kimberlyknowlezeller.com.

Erin Strybis is a freelance writer and mom of two. She spent over seven years as an editor of *Living Lutheran*, the magazine of the Evangelical Lutheran Church in America, where she edited and wrote dozens of faith stories. Erin's writing about motherhood and parenting has appeared in *The Washington Post*, *Coffee + Crumbs*, *Motherly*, *Romper*, *Bold Café*, *Gather*, *The Everymom*, and *Sparkhouse*. She lives in Chicago, Illinois. Connect with her on Instagram (@erinstrybis) and at erinstrybis.com.